Getting started with Audacity 1.3

Create your own podcasts, edit music, and more with this open source audio editor

Bethany Hiitola

[PACKT] PUBLISHING

BIRMINGHAM - MUMBAI

Getting started with Audacity 1.3

First published: March 2010

Production Reference: 1240210

Published by Packt Publishing Ltd.
32 Lincoln Road
Olton
Birmingham, B27 6PA, UK.

ISBN 978-1-847197-64-1

www.packtpub.com

Cover Image by Vinayak Chittar (vinayak.chittar@gmail.com)

Credits

Author
Bethany Hiitola

Reviewers
Arturo 'Buanzo' Busleiman
Adriano Varoli Piazza

Acquisition Editor
Sarah Cullington

Development Editor
Dhiraj Chandiramani

Technical Editor
Aaron Rosario

Indexer
Monica Ajmera Mehta

Editorial Team Leader
Akshara Aware

Project Team Leader
Priya Mukherji

Project Coordinator
Zainab Bagasrawala

Proofreader
Dirk Manuel

Production Coordinator
Adline Swetha Jesuthas

Cover Work
Adline Swetha Jesuthas

About the Author

Bethany Hiitola is a working writer. She's worked as a technical writer and multimedia developer for over 12 years, and spends the rest of her time as a wife, mother, caretaker to pets, and Master of the household. She's written more user manuals than she can count, essays, short stories, academic papers, press releases, and feature articles. And all between the day job, nap times and diaper changes. More details are available at her website: www.bethanyhiitola.com.

Without you, Matt, this book wouldn't have been possible. Thanks for watching the kids for endless hours, late nights, and into the wee mornings.

About the Reviewers

Arturo Busleiman, most commonly known as Buanzo, is a young (born in 1982) security expert (or maniac, as you prefer) who has dedicated his life to security and, as such, has been learning and working non-stop since his first line of BASIC, at the early age of eight. Today, with a lovely wife and a wonderful son, Buanzo works with new technologies, and contributes to state-of-the-art of IT security as an independent security consultant, by talking at security conferences, dictating seminars, and developing new technologies, such as Enigform and mod_openpgp (see http://wiki.buanzo.org for more information)

As an independent IT consultant, Buanzo has no employees, but a large set of people he likes working with, from all over the world, who he prefers to call friends and associates. His main partner and best friend, Bryan Slatner, is an extremely talented programmer and analyst based in North Carolina, USA. Together, there's nothing they can't achieve. Feel free to visit http://www.buanzo.com.ar/pro/eng.html for more details.

Buanzo was lucky enough to have reviewed some great books, such as *"Nmap"*, by *Gordon Fyodor Lyon, (ISBN-10: 0979958717)* and *"Computer Security: Principles and Practice"* by *William Stallings, (ISBN 0136004245)*. Additionally, he has contributed to OISSG's Information System Security Assessment Framework (Unix security), SANS TOP-20 (2003-2008), and has written many articles for Linux and security publications, such as Sys Admin Magazine (USA), SoloLinux (Spain), Linux Users (Argentina) and 2600 (USA, using a pseudonym). He's a Project Leader of the Open Web Application Security Project (OWASP).

As a member of the Audacity Team, he is in charge of system administration and security, occasionally commenting on development issues. Of course, he uses Audacity to record in his home studio. You can download some of his Audacity-recorded and mastered songs at http://blogs.buanzo.com.ar/futurabanda.

Adriano has become what he is now by both teaching himself and by paying others to do so. Although he has taken courses in Software Engineering, most of his experience in programming comes from his own interests. He's not yet a great programmer, but that's the general idea. He also has a grounding in Chemistry that started in a previous life. Adriano enjoys programming on both the LAMP and WAMP stacks, and does so for a living, creating and maintaining web applications. He wonders when will they add the Javascript J to those acronyms.

I would like to thank my lovely wife for the patience and support shown when I added a book review to an already-full schedule, and my friend Buanzo for the opportunity of reviewing for Packt. I also wish my mom was able to see this. You're always with me.

Table of Contents

Preface

This book is useful if you're new to Audacity. Using the Audacity software as a starting point, we discuss what the software is, what it can do, how you can use it, and its installation. All of this information is grounded in some basic audio editing terminology and background for those that aren't so technologically inclined.

Then we'll start digging into a sample project! You'll learn how to set up a project, create a voice track, record an interview using Skype, and also learn some basic audio editing techniques. All of this done in an easy-to-follow, task-based approach with lots of examples. Then go one step further, and teach you how to wrap all of these steps together and create a podcast that can be posted on your own website or blog.

There's always more that you can do with Audacity! The last portion of the book is dedicated to just that - discussing more advanced editing and mixing techniques, using effects, adding music, and adding additional plug-ins to the software. All of this is done incorporating examples and easy-to-follow tasks that you can try on your own audio projects. This book also provides a section on advanced editing and mixing techniques that should satisfy even experienced Audacity users. Have fun and let's get into the details so that you can get started!

What this book covers

Chapter 1, Audacity and the World of Audio Editing — From the start, we discuss what Audacity is, who typically uses it, how you can use it, and what computer operating systems it will work on. We also talk a bit about how Audacity is an open source project and what this means to you, and then we jump into learning the basics about the software: it's main screen, the menus, project window and settings for your first project.

Chapter 2, The Basics: Setting up a Project — This chapter focuses on the set up and basics about how to create a project, setting some preliminary preferences, and of course laying the ground work for your first voice track recording for a podcast.

Chapter 3, Ready and Action! Creating a Voice Track and Recording Interviews — With this chapter, it is time to actually record the podcast script, save it, and learn a few tricks about adding more to an already-recorded voice track, record additional tracks, set up a timed recording, label and delete tracks, and learn all of the details of using a third-party Internet telephony software to record telephone interviews. This is a meaty chapter, full of all of the practical instructions you need to get you really using Audacity.

Chapter 4, Making It Sound Better: Editing Your Podcast — We first discuss the basics of what digital voice waves look like, how to move around the timeline, and how to do all the basics: playback, rewinding, fast forwarding, selecting portions of the voice track, and setting up your Audacity screen to see your entire project on the screen.

Then we jump into editing details: how to cut, copy, paste, trim, delete, adjust volume levels, and silence portions of your track.

Chapter 5, Fixing the Glitches and Removing the Noise — In this chapter we get into some more advanced editing options. We see how to use filters, clean up background noises, use the equalizer, change some other sound options such as pitch, speed, and tempo and also how to normalize volumes and even out the sound across the entire audio track.

Chapter 6, Saving Projects and Exporting Podcasts — With this chapter, it is time to learn how to save your project in its final state and export it in different audio types so that you can send it as a final podcast or post it to a website for download. We'll even discuss how to use IDE tags for your podcast (artist, genre, title, and so on), the best tips and tricks for compressing your final projects into a decent file size, and preparing a file for upload to a web hosting service.

Chapter 7, Beyond the Basics: Editing for Even Better Sound — Working with the audio tracks, we can make the sounds appear more seamless, soften sibilants, clip and replace sounds, and even time-shift, all of which are more advanced editing techniques. We take a look at the steps required to use each of these techniques for any future Audacity projects that you might start.

Chapter 8, Importing and Adding Background Music — You can use Audacity to import music, convert audio files from one format to another, bring in multiple files and convert them, and more. In this chapter we will learn how to add background music into your podcast, overdub, and fade in and out. We will also look at some additional information about importing music from CDs, cassette tapes, and vinyl records.

Chapter 9, Giving your Audio some Depth: Applying Effects – Audio effects let you enhance your audio tracks. Audacity has over 20 effects that come as standard with the software. Some we will have seen in previous chapters, like Amplify, Fade In/Out, and Noise Removal, but this chapter will explain how and why you might want to use the rest.

Chapter 10, Making Audacity Even Better with Plug-ins and Libraries — Plug-ins are extra features that can be added on top of the features of Audacity. Some plug-ins can make special sound effects, or analyze audio content, and others just add to the already long list of effects already available with Audacity. The most common plug-ins for the software include: Nyquist, LADSPA, VST effects, and VAMP. We discuss how to install effects, how to use them, and why you might want to add these to your collection of effects.

Appendix A: Toolbar, Menu, and Keyboard Shortcut Reference

Appendix B: Glossary of Terms.

Who this book is for

If you are new to audio recording and editing, and particularly to the Audacity software, this book is for you. It explains everything from common audio industry terms to software basics. Technical sound engineering details and jargon are omitted, in order to keep the book beginner-friendly and easy to understand.

Conventions

New terms and **important words** are shown in bold. Words that you see on the screen, in menus or dialog boxes for example, appear in the text like this: "clicking the **Next** button moves you to the next screen".

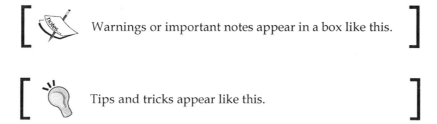

Warnings or important notes appear in a box like this.

Tips and tricks appear like this.

Reader feedback

Feedback from our readers is always welcome. Let us know what you think about this book—what you liked or may have disliked. Reader feedback is important for us to develop titles that you really get the most out of.

To send us general feedback, simply send an e-mail to feedback@packtpub.com, and mention the book title in the subject of your message.

If there is a book that you need and would like to see us publish, please send us a note via the **SUGGEST A TITLE** form on www.packtpub.com or send an e-mail to suggest@packtpub.com.

If there is a topic that you have expertise in and you are interested in either writing or contributing to a book on, see our author guide on www.packtpub.com/authors.

Customer support

Now that you are the proud owner of a Packt book, we have a number of things to help you to get the most from your purchase.

Errata

Although we have taken every care to ensure the accuracy of our content, mistakes do happen. If you find a mistake in one of our books—maybe a mistake in the text or the code—we would be grateful if you would report this to us. By doing so, you can save other readers from frustration and help us improve subsequent versions of this book. If you find any errata, please report them by visiting http://www.packtpub.com/support, selecting your book, clicking on the **let us know** link, and entering the details of your errata. Once your errata are verified, your submission will be accepted and the errata will be uploaded on our website, or added to any list of existing errata, under the Errata section of that title. Any existing errata can be viewed by selecting your title from http://www.packtpub.com/support.

Piracy

Piracy of copyright material on the Internet is an ongoing problem across all media. At Packt, we take the protection of our copyright and licenses very seriously. If you come across any illegal copies of our works, in any form, on the Internet, please provide us with the location address or website name immediately so that we can pursue a remedy.

Please contact us at copyright@packtpub.com with a link to the suspected pirated material.

We appreciate your help in protecting our authors, and our ability to bring you valuable content.

Questions

You can contact us at questions@packtpub.com if you are having a problem with any aspect of the book, and we will do our best to address it.

1
Audacity and the World of Audio Editing

This book is all about Audacity, an open source audio editing software. This means that the software is free to download, and you can use it to create items that are freely distributable. You'll learn all of the basics about creating audiocasts—or podcasts—that can be uploaded to the Web and shared with the world.

To start with, this chapter will discuss what audio editing software is, who typically uses it, how you can use it, and what computer operating systems it will work on. We'll also talk a bit about how Audacity is an open source project and what that means to you and your projects, as well as the differences between Audacity 1.2 and the latest version, in case there are a few readers who want to work with the upgrade.

 Don't worry if you're not familiar with audio terms, editing, or even recording your voice on anything other than a tape recorder. We'll go over some common audio editing terms that will get you in the know.

Also covered will be an overview of the Audacity software main screen, the main menu, main window, all of the toolbars, buttons and settings, as well as what a 'project' is in Audacity. We'll also get into some of the basic fundamentals to remember when setting up a project in Audacity. All of this will lay the foundation for your very first Audacity project of recording a podcast!

What is Audacity?

With the evolution of the Internet there has been a huge boom in personal websites, blogs, photo and music sharing sites, and things called podcasts. **Podcasts** are simple recordings of interviews, personal recollections, or entire skits, including entire entertainment "acts" that include background music and sound effects. What this change in the Internet culture has offered to the everyday person is the ability to jump into the world of audio recording. Audacity was created with this very basic need in mind.

Audacity is a simple audio editor and recorder. It can record live audio, help to convert tapes and records into digital recordings, and edit and mix a number of sound files together. What this means for you, is that you can use it to:

- **Create audiocasts or podcasts** that can be uploaded to the Web and shared with others. Podcasts can be interviews with interesting people, simple narrations, or cute snippets of your children talking.

- **Record live events** such as lectures and presentations. Of course, you need to have a laptop to bring along with you.

- **Move your old records and cassettes into the digital age** and convert them to an MP3 digital audio file. With additional equipment (a cassette or record player with a line-out plug and cable), you can connect this equipment to your computer and use Audacity to make versions of your music that you can play on a digital music player like an iPod.

- **Edit most digital audio files**, such as podcasts, to add in music, delete segments, remove unwanted noise, add in some audio effects. Audacity lets you work with audio files to make them better.

- **Record audio from YouTube**. Have you ever wanted only the audio portion of a YouTube video? Well, now you can play the video directly from YouTube, but "strip" only the audio portion out for your own use.

- **Create a ringtone for your cell phone**. Audacity lets you convert between audio formats. It supports Ogg Vorbis, MP3, WAV, and AIFF formats, and can convert between them.

It's also a great tool if you want to e-mail someone a simple audio message. Just plug in your headset, hit record, and start talking. You can have a personalized voice message that can be sent through e-mail!

Throughout this book we'll focus on one key project- creating a podcast. During this discussion there will definitely be pointers for recording events, editing audio files, and even exporting in different audio formats.

Will it work for me?

Audacity was developed by a group of volunteers under the **GNU General Public License (GPL)**, and is open source, or free software. This not only means that it does not cost anything to download, but also that you can use the program, create items with it, and freely distribute these items, modify the program itself, and share your work with others.

You can download Audacity for:

- Mac OS X
- Microsoft Windows
- GNU/Linux
- Other operating systems

Let's briefly go over how to download and install Audacity.

Windows and Mac OS

The installation process for both of these operating systems is similar:

1. Go to the official Audacity website at `http://audacity.sourceforge.net/` and download the appropriate version of the software for your computer.

2. Once the installation package has been downloaded to your computer, double-click on it to start the installation.

> For Mac computers, a DMG file is downloaded. All you need to do is uncompress that file, and drag-and-drop the **Audacity** package to the **Application** folder. For any Windows device, an EXE file is downloaded. Double-click on that file to perform the installation.

3. Find the Audacity icon (shown in the next image) in the **Application** or **Programs** folder, to open the program.

GNU/Linux

You can use Audacity with GNU/Linux operating systems (and other similar operating systems), but you should download the correct installation package for it. Currently, there are a number of distributions available for the following types of systems:

- Alt Linux
- Debian
- Fedora Core
- Fedora Project
- Mandriva i586
- OpenSUSE
- Red Hat
- SuSe and packman (suse)
- Ubuntu (http://packages.ubuntu.com/ and http://www.rpmseek.com/)

You can download the installation packages for these and others from the Audacity Linux or Unix web page, at http://audacity.sourceforge.net/download/.

In this book, the screenshots are specific to the Mac OS X software. However, don't be concerned if this is not your computer operating system of choice. The software itself is very similar between operating systems, and any notable differences between the Audacity software screens for different operating systems, are noted, so you know what to look for.

In the interest of saving you some time, there are some things that Audacity can't do in comparison to more specialized audio editing software. Audacity:

- Can't play or record files in the MIDI audio file format.
- Doesn't natively play or export audio in propriety or restricted file audio formats, such as WMA or AAC. Additional plug-ins must be installed to do this.
- Has less plug-ins and effects than a specialized **Digital Audio Workstation (DAW)**.
- Can't apply sound effects in realtime. This means that you have to record the track and then apply sound effects to the track.
- Isn't a specialized audio editing software package, so there are some limitations on multi-track editing and mixing features.

Moving up to Audacity 1.3

Audacity 1.3 offers a lot more than its predecessor, 1.2. It has some new features, which include faster equalization and noise removal tools, a new "mixer board" view with per-track volume meters, and a fullscreen view, and in addition, some basic audio information (mute, solo, gain, and track height) is now saved when you save a project.

We'll focus on Audacity version 1.3.10 in this book, including detailed keyboard shortcuts in Appendix A, *Toolbar, Menu, and Keyboard Shortcut Reference*, and the additional features afforded by the latest release.

Common audio editing terms used in Audacity

As with any new tool, there is often some terminology that comes along with understanding how it works. For Audacity, there are audio recording and editing terms that will come in handy when learning how to use the software. Some basic terms are:

- **Project** — when you open Audacity, you will open or create a new project. This includes all of the files, timing, and information on how you combined and edited different pieces of audio into your file or project. This term isn't specific to audio editing, but to software that combines pieces of different files into a single file in order to create a final output.

- **Clip** — is a short segment of audio. It can be combined with others to make an audio track.

- **Track** — one continuous audio element.

- **Library** — a collection of audio files or tracks. These can be grouped according to the content of the audio files (like a music library) or just by the location of where they are stored.

- **Effect** — there are two types of effects: generator and processing. Generator effects artificially create sounds using your audio track (or add it in). Processing effects work with the existing audio and edit or change it for a desired result.

- **Noise** — is sound of any kind, especially unintelligible or dissonant sound, that interferes with the main audio that you want heard in a track. Or simply put, it is any sound that you don't want in the audio track.

- **Bit or Sample Rates** — the number of computer bits that are conveyed or processed per unit of time. This is normally expressed in kilobits per second (kbps). A higher bit or sample rate means that your track was recorded in better quality.

- **Export**—the process of saving the audio in another format other than the format of the program that you created it in, usually so that you can play it or use it on another device or computer program. Typically, for audio, you will export files in a WAV or MP3 format.

- **WAV, AIFF, MP3**—these are all audio file types. This means that when you export an audio track from Audacity, it can be any of these formats, or you can simply do a **Save As**, to save it in the Audacity format of **AUP**. However, then only Audacity will be able to open the AUP file to listen to its contents.

As we start using Audacity and create a project, more terms will be added and explained as we move through each step. We'll be sure to call out any new terms so you can add them to your memory banks; we also collect them all in Appendix B, *Glossary of Terms* for easy reference.

Opening Audacity

No matter what operating system you use on your computer, all you need to do is find the Audacity program and open it, just as you would with any other software on your computer. The Audacity main window opens with an empty project window. This will look something like the next screenshot:

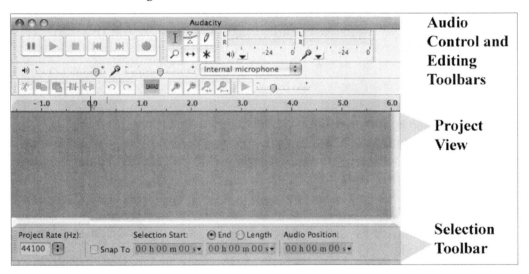

Don't be overwhelmed by this screen. Sure, there are a lot of icons and terms that might not be familiar, but we're going to review each element and how it is used. And as we begin our own sample recording session, we'll again review the icons and their use.

There are three main areas on this screen, as discussed in the following sections.

Audio controls and editing toolbars

The top portion, which includes audio controls and the many editing toolbars. These are the buttons and tools that you will use to edit and manipulate your recorded audio tracks.

Project View

The middle portion of the screen is the project view. This area will look very different when a project is open, as the timeline won't be empty. In this case it will show a digital representation of the audio that you recorded, along with some more settings that you can adjust.

Selection Toolbar

Just below the project view is the settings tool bar, which displays the frequency and bit rate information, and more timeline information, which we will cover as we start working on our sample project. But let's first discuss the main menu, and each of the toolbars on the screen.

Using the main menu

The **main menu** bar contains basic functionality for Audacity. You can open and save projects, add or hide toolbars in the main window, set preferences, as well as open the program Help file. This menu bar gives access to the entire program, even if you don't have all of the toolbars viewable.

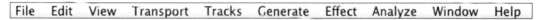

| File | Edit | View | Transport | Tracks | Generate | Effect | Analyze | Window | Help |

The main menu appears a bit differently when using different operating systems. When using Audacity on the Windows or Linux operating systems, the main menu is seen on top of the program window. With the Macintosh operating system, it is along the top bar of the computer screen.

When we begin our sample project, you'll see the most common uses of this main menu — for opening and saving Audacity project files.

Understanding the toolbars

You'll notice that on the main screen there are a number of toolbars, each with their unique icons and uses. Each of the described toolbars are displayed automatically when you first open Audacity, but the screen can also be customized for your own use by hiding some of these toolbars from the main screen. But first, let's just review each toolbar and it's constituent items at a high level, so that you can become familiar with Audacity and it's simple interface.

Control Toolbar

Most prominent on the screen is the **Control Toolbar**. This should look very familiar, in that it contains common icons that are used for any audio device: Play, Pause, Record, Skip to Start, Skip to End, and Stop. These are the basic controls for recording and playing back the sound that you record using Audacity.

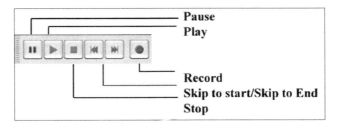

In fact, if you are anxious to try the software out, let's learn a bit about the **Mixer Toolbar**, in order to perform a simple set up and sample recording.

Mixer Toolbar

The **Mixer Toolbar** is all about setting the volume and choosing the recording device. On the left-hand side (the speaker icon), you can adjust the input volume levels. In the middle, to the right of the microphone icon, you can adjust the volume of the output that you'd like your audio track to have.

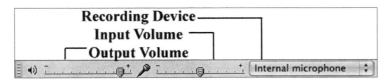

On the right-hand side, you can choose the device that you'd like to use to make the recording. As you can see in the previous screenshot, we use an internal microphone (the one that is pre-installed on the computer that we are using), but you could also choose to use an external microphone or other recording device as the input.

Changing any of these settings is as simple as using your mouse to adjust the volumes, or clicking on the drop-down box to change the recording device. If you want a specific value for your volumes, you can also double-click on the volume scale to open a window where you can enter a specific audio level value.

Give it a try!

Ready to try out the software? Then go back to the **Control Toolbar** and click on the **Record** button. Start speaking into your computer's internal microphone (that is, if you computer or laptop has one! If not, connect a microphone to the USB or input port). Click on the **Stop** button when you are finished. You've just completed your first test recording session! It's as simple as that to record voice tracks. Click on the **Play** button to review your first composition!

Tools Toolbar

The **Tools Toolbar** gives you some control options in the recorded audio's timeline. It is not as complicated as it sounds. When you record some audio, the digital translation of that appears in the project view portion of the Audacity screen. Then select one of these tools and you are able to manipulate the recorded audio track. You can select specific sections of the audio track, zoom into the details to delete any unwanted noise, fade in and out at the beginning or end of tracks, shift audio clips on the timeline (which is particularly important if you are adding an introduction or exit), and work to select and replicate certain sounds.

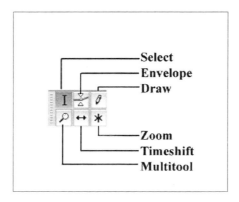

Let's give it a try. Use the **Selection Tool** I to "highlight" a portion of the test track that you sampled when you first opened the program, as seen in the next screenshot:

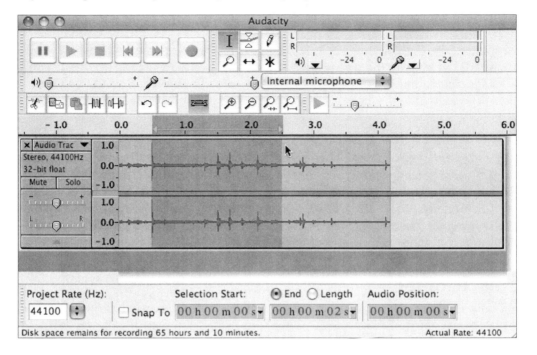

All you need to do is use your mouse to activate the **Selection Tool**, and then click-and-drag the mouse across the timeline, releasing the mouse button when you want to stop selecting. The "selected" portion of the audio track will appear in a darker shade of gray, as seen in the previous screenshot. Try it a few times to get a feel of how you make selections.

You use selections to make changes to only a specific portion of the audio track. For example, if you wanted what you selected here to be louder than the rest of the track, keep this portion selected, and then go to the main menu and select **Effect** and then **Amplify**. You'll see the audio waves in that area increase, indicating that the volume of this portion is now much higher.

Let's also give one of the other edit tools a try. Select the **Zoom Tool**, and drag your mouse over the area and click on it. The timeline intervals decrease to show you even more detail of the audio waves that were recorded.

You can also select any of the other tools and perform the same action (clicking on the audio track).

Meter Toolbar

Simply put, the **Meter Toolbar** displays the mono or stereo channels of your audio track. As an example, when recording a song, different instruments are placed in different channels. So in this example, there are mono (1) or stereo (2) channels in which we can record audio for our tracks.

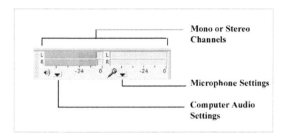

You can select preferences, and even disable certain inputs, by clicking on the down arrow icons near the microphone or speaker settings. However, the inputs (and outputs) listed in these fields are dependent on what hardware or peripheral items you have connected and installed on your computer. Feel free to take a look at what settings are available here.

This toolbar also displays input levels. The green bars move during recording or playback, to show the volume levels. So they move higher (to the right) when the recording or playback is louder. Peaks in the volume, or the highest volume reached when recording are also indicated here, by a small line. This can be useful when editing later, if you see a peak point, but if most of the volume levels are below that point throughout the rest of the track, then you might need to normalize the entire audio track.

Edit Toolbar

Probably the most useful toolbar is the **Edit Toolbar**. This will be one of the most used toolbars when we work through our sample project.

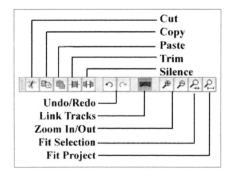

Once a track has been recorded and is displayed in the project window, the items on this toolbar become active. You can cut pieces out of the audio tracks, paste new items in, trim, link, and silence any unwanted noise. This toolbar also lets you undo your last editing option, zoom into a certain area of the recorded track, and adjust the viewing window so that it works with your preferences. You can even fit the audio tracks to your window size.

For example, with your test recording, use the **Selection Tool** from the **Tools Toolbar** to select a small portion of the audio track. Then select **Cut** from the **Edit** menu. Did that portion of the track disappear? If so, select **Undo**, and you should see the selection re-appear in your audio timeline. You will see details on each of these items as we work through our sample project in this book.

Transcription Toolbar

A toolbar for more advanced editing features is the **Transcription Toolbar**. This toolbar helps you to speed up or slow down playback for the the selected audio in your timeline.

Using this toolbar is as easy as using the **Selection Tool** to highlight a portion of an audio track, and then using the scale to slow down (move the marker to the left) or speed up (move the marker to the right) the audio. Conveniently, you can also use the green **Play** button to play back the selected portion, to check if you have the correct playback speed.

Again, if you'd rather set a specific value for the playback speed, double-click the scale and a window is displayed that lets you you enter a number for the playback speed.

Selection Toolbar

The **Selection Toolbar** is at the bottom of the Audacity main window—just below the project window. Its most common use is to set the **Project Rate** (commonly measured in Hertz). Technically, it measures the number of computer bits that are conveyed or processed per unit of time. The higher the sample rate, the better the quality of the recording. The sample rate used by audio CDs is 44100 Hz, and this is the default in Audacity and is by far the most common sample rate for most audio recordings.

You can also use the **Snap To** feature, which allows you to have specific settings for when a new clip of audio starts. So, for example, if you wanted this audio track to align with some video content, then you can exactly match the visual frame timing with this audio. This is an advanced feature of the software, and can be adjusted for various time formats and settings.

When the **Snap To** box is checked, it is considered active, and the remaining fields also become active. You can choose a particular unit of measurement (in the example, the format is in hours : minutes : seconds), and the format is changed for all three display ranges at a time. You can choose between **End** and **Length** for the second field. **Audio Position** is shown in the third field, and shows the current cursor position, and also allows you to manually set it.

As you work more with Audacity and you need to do more precise audio editing, these **Snap To** fields will be important in creating a clean audio track.

Understanding projects

To start working in Audacity, you must open a project. By default, when you open Audacity for the very first time, it is a new project—and the screen looks noticeably blank. But before we start jumping into the details of project creation, it is important to understand what a project is.

A project is not the end-product or output from Audacity. It is actually a working draft of all of the work that you have done on the collection of files that you imported and used in the creation of a final file.

Project files, when saved in Audacity, are AUP files. AUP is the default file format when you choose **File** and then **Save Project** from the main menu.

A project encompasses all of the clips and files that you have already imported into Audacity, the timing, silencing, and other editing that you have spent time to create. All of this, is stored in a way that Audacity recognizes. So the next time you open your AUP project file, it's all there, just the way you saved it.

If you were now to save the test sample recording that you made at the very beginning of this chapter, by selecting **File** and then **Save Project** from the main menu, then you would be prompted for a file name, and would notice that the file will be saved as an AUP file. You could then reopen this file, edit it some more, fade in the sound, cut or trim the clip, and then save your changes. The next time you open this file, all of those edits would still be applied.

Pointers for working in Audacity

Whenever you work with Audacity, there are some rules that you should remember that will make your projects run a little bit more smoothly. These include:

- **There is one audio clip per track.** Remember that a clip is simply a piece of audio that is imported, recorded, split, or duplicated from another track.

- **A track, on the other hand, is one continuous piece of audio (as shown in your timeline).** This means that it can only carry one piece of audio at a time. You can add to an audio track by pasting audio into it, inserting silence, or cutting a piece away, but it will always be one continuous piece of audio.

- **Audacity always records to a new track.** When you click on **Record**, this will always be a new audio track to work with. The new track will appear at the bottom of the project view. Sometimes you may need to resize the Audacity window, or scroll to the bottom-most audio track in order to see what was, or is being, recorded.

- **Audacity references the original audio until you actually perform an edit, cut, silence, or apply some sort of audio effect to it.** But note that if you are ever unhappy with an edit, you can always undo (and then, if necessary, redo) all of the edits that you have made, even after you have saved your project.

Using the best equipment

To get the best sound, you need a good microphone. But let's keep this in perspective. It is your first time using Audacity and creating a podcast, right? So our project doesn't need to be professional in its quality of sound. Any microphone will do the trick, including any internal microphone that your computer may have. However, it is worth recommending some microphone options that will make editing and cleaning up the vocal tracks easier. For any future projects, you may want to upgrade your equipment—because a better microphone, sound card, and audio setup will record your audio with much less degradation up front. When you compress your recording to create an MP3, your recording will sound better, and will also require less of your time for post-production.

Generally, here's what you'll need:

- A computer (or laptop) with a sound card
- A microphone
- A microphone stand, or something to secure the microphone while you are recording, may be useful, so that you can avoid any additional interference

Sound cards

The sound card allows your computer to record audio. There are hundreds of sound card varieties, some with many "lines in" for recording multiple items at once (say, if you're part of a band and want each instrument to have an individual microphone) or just one input. Others have microphones bundled with the product, and there are even a few that include additional useful software packages, including Audacity. Again, for our project, any sound card will do, as long as it has a line-in and is functional. For ongoing projects, you should research the best sound cards for the best recording quality, depending on what will best fit your needs.

Microphones

For the microphone option, there are several different types to consider in the long run, depending on what you are recording, your other equipment, and the purpose that your audio track will serve. Your range of choices is as follows:

- The most inexpensive option is to use your computer's internal microphone (if it has one). This is definitely enough to get you started on our sample project.

- The next least-expensive option is a simple headset of the kind that are easily available in most big department stores, and are used commonly by computer gamers. The headphone portion uses your computer's sound card and lets you listen to stereo sound from music, games, movies, and more. The microphone, is usually incorporated into the headset, is often noise-canceling, and generally offers decent quality sound recording. With a headset, no microphone stand or other equipment is required to get started.

- The next best choice is a dynamic microphone. They are durable, with few moving parts, and are ideal for someone who wants that little bit of extra quality when recording vocals. No additional power source is needed, but a microphone stand is recommended.

In addition to these basic options, there are several other varieties of microphones that vary in both price and the quality of sound that they record. However, many of these will require even more equipment to work effectively. Hence, sticking to the basics will get you through your project.

Summary

You should now be ready to get started! You've learned what audio editing software is, and about Audacity in particular, its capabilities, and what it can (and can't) do for your audio projects. We've also covered how to download the Audacity software, what operating systems it works on, and what version is best for you.

You've just begun the journey into audio editing with Audacity by skimming over some basic audio editing terms that will be useful. We even covered the basics of the Audacity main screen, the main menu, each toolbar, an overview of each button, field, and setting, and have learnt about Audacity projects. You were even able to test some of the buttons and menus, when recording a very simple test audio track. Also, we covered some basic pointers, or things to remember when working with Audacity (all the little details about how we can or can't manipulate an audio track) and a handful of equipment pointers. All this in an effort to give us a foundation for creating a simple podcast, which is coming up next!

2

The Basics: Setting Up a Project

Having learnt the basics of Audacity and all of its tools in the main window, it's now time to get started with a project. In this chapter you'll learn how to create a new project, set your preliminary preferences, choose quality settings, and determine how you will export your project when it is complete. You'll even start planning your first recording session.

Creating a new project

When you open Audacity for the first time, it automatically opens a new, empty project. To begin, you'll want to make sure that you give the project it's own name and folder location for file management purposes. Then you'll know where the files are saved and stored for your project. To do this is simple: from the main menu, select **File** and then **Save Project As**.

File	Edit	View	Transport	Tracks
New				⌘N
Open...				⌘O
Open Recent				▶
Close				⌘W
Save Project				⌘S
Save Project As...				
Save Compressed Copy of Project...				
Check Dependencies...				
Open Metadata Editor...				
Import				▶

The **Save As** window is displayed, prompting you for a filename for your project. Type a file name, and then click on **Save**.

You'll notice that there are now two files in your save location: an AUP file with your project name, and a directory or folder named project name_data.

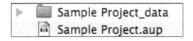

The .aup file is the Audacity-specific project file, and is what you would select to reopen your project once you have closed it. The _data folder is exactly as it is named— a data directory that Audacity uses to store all of the recorded audio and changes that you make to the .aup file.

Remember, these are file names and types that only Audacity recognizes. Once you have recorded and edited your audio to make it sound its best, you will **Export** and save into a common audio format like MP3.

As you work in Audacity, recording, editing, and working on your audio track, it is always good practice to save your project often, so that you don't lose any of your hard work. This is as easy as clicking on **File,** and then selecting **Save Project** from the main menu.

Save shortcut keys

You can also use the **Save Project** shortcut keys on your keyboard when you want to save your project. For the Windows operating system you would use *Ctrl + S*. Within MAC OS X, use *Command + S*.

Setting the Audacity Preferences

Now that your project has a name and is saved on your computer, you need to set up the project so it will perform as expected when it is complete. You do this by setting up the project **Preferences**. Go to the main menu and select **Audacity** and then **Preferences**.

When using a computer running the Microsoft Windows or Linux operating systems, you can find the preferences in the main menu. Look for **Preferences** under enter the **Edit** or the **File** menu.

There are many options on this screen. The most crucial to your project are:

- Devices
- Quality
- Import / Export

Select any one of the preferences to see the settings for that option.

Verifying playback and recording settings

On the **Devices** preferences screen, you want to pay attention to the **Playback Device** and **Recording Device** settings. Click on **Devices** to view these options, as seen in the next screenshot.

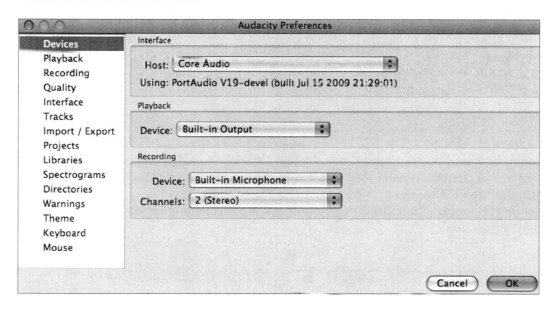

If you are using an external microphone such as a headset, headpiece, or a dynamic microphone, make sure that the **Device** option under **Recording** is set to the external microphone.

You may also want to check the **Channels** option, under **Recording**. If you're going to record a stereo signal, then you need to make sure **Channels** is set to **2 (Stereo)**.

Again, for our sample project, using an internal or built-in microphone (as shown in the previous screenshot) and your computer speakers is just fine. In fact, they are most likely the easiest and cheapest solution.

Quality settings check

The **Quality** preferences allow you to set the sample rate of the recording. Click on **Quality** in the **Audacity Preferences** screen to view these options.

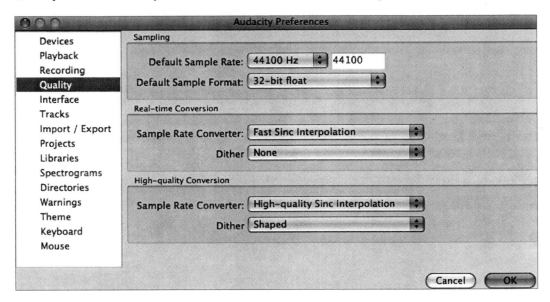

The default audio sample rate in Audacity is 44100 Hz, which is the most common sample rate for audio recording. You can leave these settings as they are for the sample project. However, if you want to buff up the quality of your recording, this is where you change the sample rate before you start recording, to get the best sound quality possible.

Setting up for importing and exporting

Lastly, the **Import / Export** preferences are important so that you can set how you will edit your audio track. To access this screen, click on **Import / Export** on your **Audacity Preferences** screen.

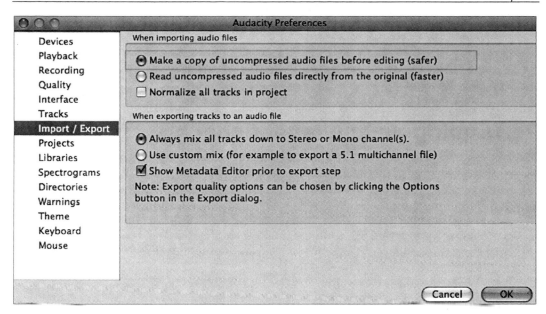

The top portion of this screen has preferences for importing additional audio. These options are particularly useful if you plan on adding some background music, introduction, or closing music. When importing audio files, Audacity is set to **Read uncompressed audio files directly from the original** (the second option) by default. As the option states, this is the fastest option for your computer. However, if for any reason you delete your original audio file, there is no way to get it back.

If you choose to make a copy of all imported audio (so that it is saved in your _data file), it will take up more hard drive space on your computer. However, it also affords you the best way to back up a project and recover from any accidental errors that may occur.

Why must we make this decision now? This is the only time to adjust this setting. Even if you don't intend to import any additional audio, you might want to take a few moments to adjust this setting to plan for any future uses of this project.

For our sample project, let's change the setting to **Make a copy of uncompressed audio files before editing**. We'll be importing additional audio to our recording as we move through the project. This way we'll not have to worry about losing any of our project pieces, and will be able to recover any lost work.

With the preferences set, we are ready to plan our final details.

Planning for your recording session

Planning for your recording session will help with the editing process. You'll have the best audio from your recording equipment, and possibly speed up the entire recording session. Let's discuss your equipment first.

Performing an equipment check

It's always good practice to make sure that all connections, wires, and inputs are secure and set up properly before you begin. Not only will this make for a smoother recording session, but it will ensure that audio is actually captured when you click on record!

If you are using an external microphone, make sure that the line is connected to the microphone input or line-in connector of your sound card. It is then time to test.

Most sound cards are pretty simple to test. Plug in the microphone, open your sound card mixer (the software that came with the sound card or is included in the operating system of your computer), and start speaking into the microphone.

For Microsoft Windows, the mixer is under the **Control Panel | Sound**. For Mac, open the **System Preferences** and select **Sound** to open the control panel. For Linux, it is likely that you will have to use a separate third-party application for this test.

Next, for all operating systems, select **Input** to see, adjust, and test your sound levels.

Because we plan to use an internal microphone and sound card for our sample project (at least for those of us that have that option), just open your sound control panel or preferences and test your microphone. If you tried recording in Audacity as described in the previous chapter, and were able to record your voice, you've already performed a mike check!

Positioning your microphone

For this sample project, we're simply trying out Audacity, so there is no real need to get technical and try to find the best place, grip, or stand for your microphone, whether internal or external. However, a few good pointers can't hurt, especially if you decide to do more Audacity projects in the future. So, here are a few helpful hints:

- For internal microphones, there isn't much that you can do about placement, in order to reduce ambient noise. Just make sure that your computer is not closed-in or very close to corners in a room.

- If you're using an external microphone, a microphone stand helps to reduce noise. Otherwise, your hand tightening or loosening its grip on the base of the microphone, moving it during the conversation, and so on, will add noise to the recording. You can try suspending the microphone, so that the microphone hangs down in front of your mouth when you speak. That way, it isn't lying on any surfaces that will reflect sound, and this can help to eliminate some additional noise while you are talking.

- Make sure that during your recording session you are in a quiet area.

Planning a podcast

As stated, our sample project will be to record a podcast. So, what are you going to record? To make it simple, you could take a book from your night stand, or today's newspaper, and pick a story to read for one or two minutes. That should be plenty of material, and will probably also include some noise interruptions for us to edit.

If you want to be more formal, you could create an original podcast. Typical podcasts have three parts: an introduction, the content of the podcast (the information or interview), and the exit or ending. Each of these could either be scripted (typed or written) in a way that would be easy for you to read while being recorded, or done impromptu. Just be cautious when flying by the seat of your pants, as you may find yourself saying *umm*, *ahhh*, or *oooh* a lot while talking. All of these can be cut out during editing, but too many "thought" noises will make for a choppy podcast. An audience likes to hear narrations, stories, and information, not the extra fillers.

No matter what you choose—a formal podcast, reading from a recent story, or something impromptu—it is highly recommended that you familiarize yourself with what you will be discussing. Practice a few times. Re-read the story thrice, or more, and definitely create some questions (if you are conducting an interview) ahead of time, so that when you press record, you're ready to start. Not only will this help the quality of the podcast, it will also help your speaking techniques for when you are live and recording.

Summary

We spent a lot of time discussing your recording equipment in this chapter, including the best microphone and sound card options, as well as how to test all of this equipment for it's first use. All of this was in preparation for the first sample project, which we created, set the preferences for, and saved to our computer. We even did a bit of planning to decide what we'll start recording, which will be handy in the next chapter.

3
Ready and Action! Creating a Voice Track and Recording Interviews

In the previous chapter, we began a project, set some initial preferences, got the equipment set up, and even discussed the content for our podcast. Now it's time to actually record the script, save it, and learn some tricks about adding more to an already-recorded voice track, record additional tracks, set up a timed recording, label and delete tracks, and learn all the details of using third-party internet telephony software to record telephone interviews. This chapter provides some practical instructions to get you started using Audacity to record voice tracks.

Recording voice tracks

With your material—script, story, or notes—you're ready to go, right? We shall start with a standard manual recording session.

The simple voice track

This is the simplest recording session. When you're ready, carry out the steps below:

1. Open the Audacity project that you created in the previous chapter (if it isn't already open) on your computer.

2. Take a deep breath, and then click on the **Record** button, as seen in the next screenshot, and start speaking aloud your script.

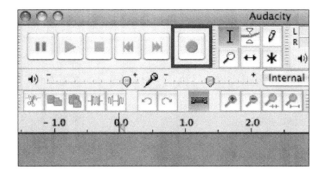

3. Immediately, you'll see the project view portion of your Audacity window change. A voice track will appear, showing your recording, live!

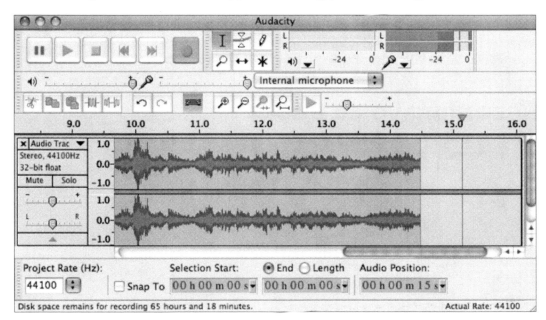

4. The left (**L**) and right (**R**) channels show the volume of your voice (shown in the bars in the upper-right-hand of the previous screenshot). The digital interpretation of your voice is shown in the audio track portion of the project view (the blue "lines", or sound waves, that you see on your screen). Don't let this make you nervous; just focus on delivering a great voice track.

5. Keep reading your script or sample piece as naturally as possible.

6. When you're done, click on the **Stop** button.

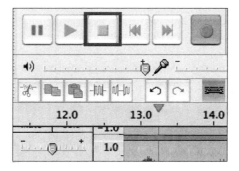

7. As soon as you click on the **Stop** button, you'll see that the recording stops, all activity in Audacity stops, and recording is over.

8. Save your track to the project folder so that you'll be ready to start editing it. From the main menu, select **File** and then **Save Project**.

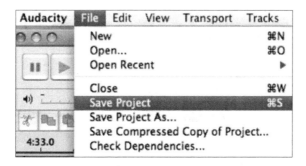

Recording Tip

Keep any paper (your notes or script) in a place that won't interrupt the recording session when you flip the pages — preferably away from the microphone, or already spread out in front of you so that you can refer to them without touching them. We will learn how to "silence" these sounds later on, but having a clean initial recording always makes it a little easier.

That's it, you've just completed your first recording session with Audacity! It really is as simple as that. But, as with the first time I used the software, I know there are likely things that you would like to change.

So let's discuss some additional techniques for recording voice tracks.

Adding to a voice track

When you first install Audacity, it is set to always start a new voice track session each time that you click on **Record** by default. This means that, right now, after just finishing your first full recording session, if you clicked on the **Record** button again, it would start a new voice track below the one that you just recorded (giving you another set of blue lines in the project view, as shown in the next example).

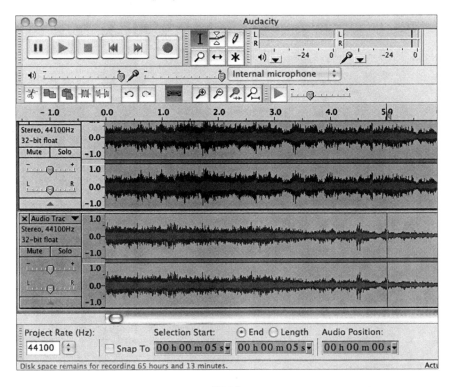

You can change one setting so that you can add to a voice track that has already been recorded. Technically, this is called **appending** a voice track. Once this option has been set, recording will automatically begin at the end of where the previous voice track ended (as seen in the next screenshot).

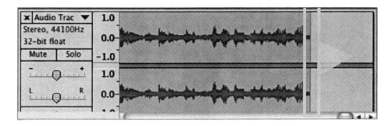

You can set up Audacity to append to an existing recording as follows:

1. First, in the Audacity project view, select the voice track to which you want to add content. This is important because immediately after you perform the next step, Audacity will be recording.

2. In the main menu, click on **Transport** and then select **Append Record**. Audacity begins recording immediately.

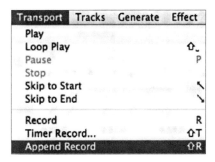

3. When you are done appending the voice track, click on the **Stop** button.

Similarly, you can always record a separate voice track that begins where the first ends, and then combine them manually. This is essentially the same as appending, and may be a bit easier to do.

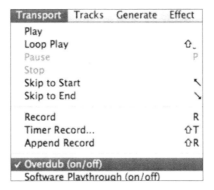

To record an audio track that follows a prior recording, there is a setting that you need to change. By default, Audacity has overdubbing set to **On**. To turn this off, use the following steps:

1. Go to the main menu, and select **Transport** and then **Overdub**. You'll notice that the check mark will disappear. This means that overdubbing is turned off.

To record an audio track that follows a prior recording, there is a setting that you need to change.

 You'll learn more about overdubbing—what it is, how you would use it, and more–in Chapter 8, *Importing and Adding Background Music*.

2. Next, go to the audio track timeline into which you want to insert this new recording. Place your cursor on the timeline where you want the new recording to start, and then click on it.

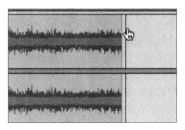

3. Next, click on the **Record** button. Recording will start right away, at the exact timeline location that you selected.

4. When you are done, click on the **Stop** button to stop recording.

5. To play the entire sequence—the first and second tracks together—just click on the beginning of the timeline, and then click on the **Play** button.

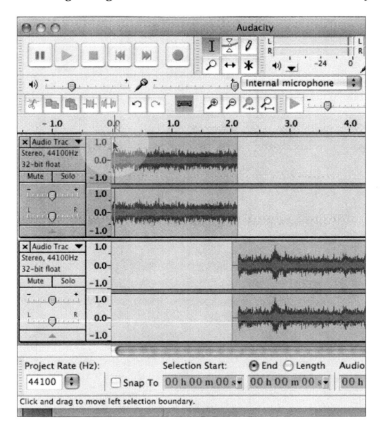

[Always remember that the timeline begins at the **0.0** mark which is likely to be at the beginning of the first audio track.]

Always keep in mind that audio is recorded and played back based on a timeline in Audacity. So in this case, it starts at **0.0** and moves forward. Tracks that you record on the same timeline will play in parallel. You can use this to overdub, or record another track "on top" of what you have already recorded (say for background music) when you want to. More on overdubbing shortly. Let's first discuss how you can label recorded audio tracks for easy identification.

Labeling recorded audio tracks

Now that you have an audio track or two recorded and present in the Audacity project view screen, let's give them proper names so we can tell them apart and prepare them for future editing work. To label a track, click on the down arrow to the far left of that track's timeline, and select **Name** from the context menu.

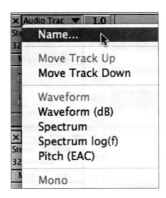

A new window will appear, containing a field in which you can enter the name of the audio track.

Do this for each audio track that you have recorded so far. Be descriptive here, so that you know at a glance if this is an introduction track, or just an added explanation for the story you just told. The next time that you open this project file, it will be helpful to know what each track is without having to play it back over and over. This is especially important when you work with large projects.

To be on the safe side, let's save our work again. Go to the main menu, and select **File** and then **Save Project**.

Deleting an audio track

There may be a time when you record an additional audio track and then decide that it didn't work out well, or that it is extraneous. It's very easy to delete tracks. Directly to the left-hand side of the track name is a small **X** (close) button. Click on this button to delete the track from the timeline.

 Just remember that when you click on the close button, there is no recovering that audio track. It is deleted permanently.

An alternative to deleting the track would be to just mute the track (click on the **Mute** button below the close button). The track then remains within the project, but won't be heard during playback, and can be un-muted at any time.

Recording an interview with Skype

If you are interested in doing more than solo podcasts with Audacity, you can always try creating interview podcasts. You can record these live in your office with your computer's internal microphone, or with additional microphones. However, you can't always perform an interview from the comfort of your office due to conflicting schedules and the location of your interviewee. Hence, let's learn how to record an interview using your phone and your computer.

First you'll need to install another software that allows you to make phone calls using your computer. The program we are going to use for this example is Skype. However, you could use other software that does the same thing for your Internet telephony set-up.

Download and install Skype

Skype is software that allows us to make voice calls over the Internet, particularly to other users of Skype. Some numbers (such as toll-free numbers) are free of charge, while calls to landlines and mobile phones may require a small fee.

 For details on pricing for Skype credits for landline and cell calls go to: http://www.skype.com/.

Let's briefly discuss how to download and install Skype.

1. First, go to http://www.skype.com/ and download the appropriate version of the software for your computer.

2. Once the installation package has been downloaded to your computer, double-click on it to begin the installation.

 For Mac computers, a .DMG file is downloaded. All you need to do is uncompress that file and drag-and-drop the **Skype** package to the **Application** folder. For any Windows device, an .exe file is downloaded. Double-click on that file to begin the installation. For Linux, there are multiple distributions available.

3. If you aren't already prompted to do so, start the Skype application and follow the on-screen instructions to sign up for a new Skype account.

4. Once you have registered and signed in, the main Skype screen is displayed, which should look similar to the next screenshot:

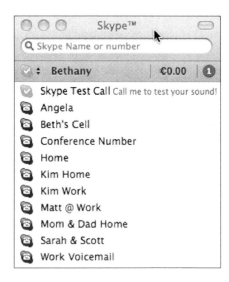

Set up Skype for your telephone interview

For our project, we've been using the computer's internal microphone, so there shouldn't be any additional set up in either Skype or Audacity. However, to be sure you may want to check the recording input devices in Audacity to make sure that you can record both sides of the interview. To do this, use the following steps:

1. In the Audacity window, go to the main menu, and then select **Audacity** and then **Preferences**.

 When using a computer running the Microsoft Windows or Linux operating systems, you can find these preferences from the main menu. Select **File** and then **Preferences**.

2. In the **Audacity Preferences** window, select **Devices**.

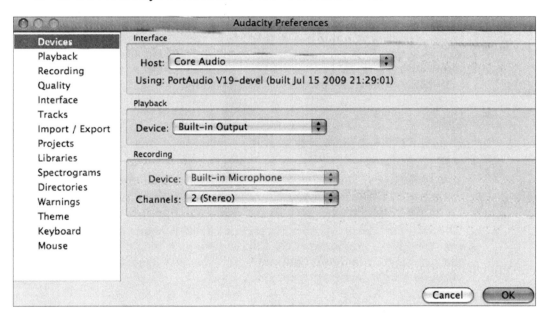

3. Check the **Device** settings under **Recording**. Particularly if you are using multiple inputs, it may be best to select **Stereo Mixer** or similar input.

 If there are many devices listed with the **Recording | Device** drop-down menu, perform a few interview tests with a friend on Skype prior to the recording session, to determine which of the connected devices will actually be doing the recording.

You might also want to turn off all notifications in Skype. These are all of the alert sounds for events such as contacts logging in and out, incoming call alerts, and so on. To do this, follow the steps shown below:

1. Open Skype and log in.

2. From the main menu, select **Skype** and then **Preferences**.

3. Select the **Notifications** tab.

4. Be sure to uncheck the **Play Sound** checkbox. This will make sure that all sounds are suspended and won't interrupt your recording session.

Recording the Skype call

When you are ready to begin your interview, use the following steps to call the other party:

If this is the first time that you've used Skype you will probably have to add a few people to your contact list. It's easy; on the main menu, select **Contacts** and then **Add a Contact**. Then enter the contact name and telephone number, and then click on **Add Number**.

1. Open Skype.

2. In the main window, double-click on the contact to initiate a call.

Get creative! With Skype you don't need to limit yourself to only one other person on the call. Skype allows you to start a conference call with up to five people (yourself included).

To start a conference call, open Skype, and on the main menu choose **Call** and then **Start a Conference Call**. On a computer running Windows, you can just click on the **Conference** button, and then select the individuals that you want to include on your call.

3. Once everyone is on the call, yourself included, start recording your conversation. In the Audacity window on your computer, click on the **Record** button and begin your interview. You should see the digital interpretation of your interview (the blue lines that move with the timelines) in the **Project View** of the Audacity screen, just like when you recorded a simple audio voice track.

4. When you're done, click on the **Stop** button to stop recording.

5. Finally, don't forget to hang up your Skype call! Click on the red **Hang Up** button in the active call window.

For better volume control

Before you begin recording, you may want to use the Audacity volume control panel to adjust the audio inputs to similar levels (wave and microphone) so that it is consistent for a listener.

As seen in the previous screenshot, the bars give a visual indication of the current audio levels in Audacity.

1. The set of bars on the left-hand side shows output volume levels (these are in green); the right-hand side set are the input volume levels (these are shown in red).

2. You measure volume levels from left to right, with the far left being silence, and the further right it moves, the louder the audio.

3. In stereo recording, the top bar is the left channel and bottom bar is the right.

4. When recording, you will see that the bars vary in brightness and will show different indicators or markers. The brightest portion of the bar displays the average audio volume level. The darkest part of the bar shows the highest (peak) audio level.

5. The small line or marker shown in the rightmost portion in the bar is the highest audio level recorded in the last 3 seconds of recording.

6. If **clipping** occurs (audio becomes distorted), an indicator in the far right is displayed. This can be remedied by stopping the recording session, lowering the volume of the input, and then resuming recording.

Using timed recordings

There might be times when you want to set up a timed recording session, instead of having to manually click on the **Record** and **Stop** buttons. This can be useful if you are setting up a chat through a conference call for many parties at an agreed upon predetermined time, like a chat with a famous author or celebrity, and you want to pay attention to the conversation. To set one up prior to the call, use the following steps:

1. In the Audacity window, go to the main menu, select **Transport** and then **Timer Record**.

2. The **Timer Record** window appears with **Start and End date and time** fields, along with a **Duration** field. These are very precise, so set them for your call time with a bit of overage, just in case the conversation gets lengthy. After that, click on **OK**.

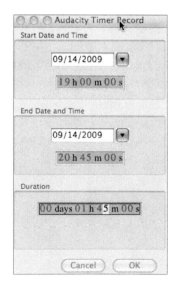

A **Waiting for Start** window appears, as seen in the next screenshot. This shows the time until the time-recording will start, as well as a way to cancel the auto-record option. You can step away from your computer for a short time, but just be sure you return before your call, as Audacity will automatically start recording at that time.

Just remember: don't turn off your computer or allow it to go into sleep mode during the call or recording session!

Once it is time for the recording to begin, you can make your Skype call, or just sit down and get ready to start talking. Audacity will start recording until the allotted time is up.

Summary

We spent this entire chapter describing everything that you need to know about recording voice tracks and interviews. We learned the basics of a recording session and how to save it. We also learned how to append to the initial recording, add another recorded track within the timeline (or immediately after it), recording additional tracks to merge, setting up a timed recording, and the steps to label tracks for organization, or to delete them. You learnt all of this, plus the details of using a third party internet telephony software such as Skype to record telephone interviews. Now it's time to learn how to edit and enhance those voice tracks to make them sound even better!

4
Making It Sound Better: Editing Your Podcast

With the recording session over, it's now time to get down to the editing. We'll first discuss the basics of what digital voice waves look like, how to move around in the timeline, and all the basics, such as playback, rewinding, fast forwarding, selecting portions of the voice track, and setting up Audacity so that you can see your entire project on the screen.

Then we're going to jump into editing details about how to cut, copy, paste, trim, delete, adjust volume levels, and silence portions of your track. Obviously, your voice track may not need every one of these items done to it, but we'll cover all of them. As you use Audacity more, this will give you the basics for almost any editing that needs to be done after a recording session.

Dissecting the recorded audio

As you were recording your podcast in the previous chapter, you may have seen blue lines or "waves" (as seen in the next screenshot) moving across your screen as you were speaking.

In the simplest form, these are your voice waves being converted to a digital form and displayed by Audacity on your screen. We're not going to go into all the details of voice waves—it may well be an entire science lesson in itself—but let's take a look at the very basic parts of what you recorded: the "levels" of the digital voice waves and how you can interpret them visually. This will help us to better understand how we can edit our podcast for "cleaner" audio.

Voice waves

The entire sequence of waves on the screen can be overwhelming to look at, but we'll take it bit by bit. First, look closely at your recorded audio. You'll see distinct groups of waves that are larger than the others. These "larger" groups of waves are the portions of the recording where you are speaking words, and are called **voice waves**.

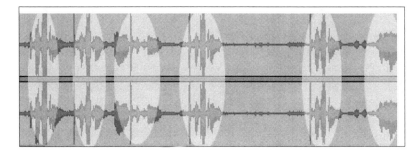

As you move horizontally across the track, you'll see that these waves vary in height (which translates into louder elements) and width (groups of words).

Silence

The portions of the voice track that don't show large waves of voice, are considered **silences**. How silent these portions actually are depends on how noisy an environment you are recording in. But generally, silences are shown as straight lines, as seen in the next screenshot.

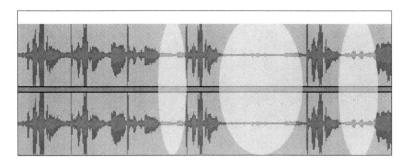

Combined with the voice waves, you can now visually "see" the speaking portions of the track, and the portions where there are breaks. This is important because as we move through editing you can apply any number of effects on each part of the recorded track.

Along with the effects, voice portions can be amplified (increased in volume), cut, deleted, duplicated, and trimmed. Silences can also be cut, deleted, or trimmed, depending on how you want entire track to sound as a whole. We'll discuss all of these later on, but let's first review some basic tools, and how to use them.

Timeline

The timeline follows the horizontal of the audio track. Specifically, it shows a measurement of time for the entire length of the track. On the Audacity screen, when an audio track is displayed in the project view, you'll see numbers along the top of the audio track, as seen in the next screenshot.

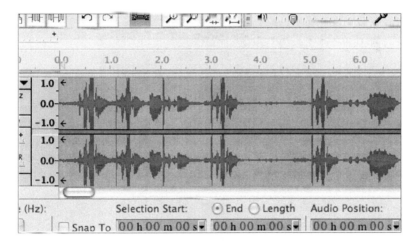

As you move horizontally through the recording, the timeline increments in one second intervals. We'll discuss how to "zoom in" on the audio track, which will allow you to see even further detailed timelines—down to the millisecond or smaller— and edit out any noise. This timeline offers precision when you are trying to merge tracks, paste in new audio, or even delete a word in a sentence.

Working within the project

As you begin editing in Audacity, you'll need to review your changes, and make sure that your recording sounds exactly the way that you want it to. Here's the basics on playback, rewinding, fast forwarding, selecting, magnifying, and adjusting project views in Audacity.

Playback

You'll become very familiar with your audio track as you listen to, and edit it. After each change, you'll likely want to play it back to make sure that it sounds just right. To play back the track (or a portion of it), simply click on the **Play** button.

Not hearing playback?

It's possible that you're stuck at the end of your audio track. Click on the **Skip to Start** button move to the beginning of the timeline, and then click on the **Play** button.

As you begin your edit, you'll play back your audio track many times over, as you adjust and make changes to get it just right. Try listening to the playback on headphones, as well as separately on a set of external speakers. All of this playback on different equipment should give you a slightly different experience every time, and will allow you to optimize your audio tracks for both speaker and headphone playback.

Rewinding and fast forwarding

As your audio tracks get longer, you won't always want to listen to the entire track. You can just move your mouse forward or back in the timeline and click where you want to start listening from.

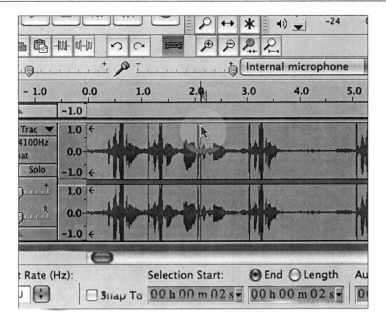

Once the cursor is in place, click on the **Play** button. The playback will continue until the end of the track, or until you click on the **Stop** button.

Alternatively, you can always click on the **Skip to Start** button to start at the beginning of the track.

Selecting portions of your track

There will be many times when you only want to play, view, or manipulate a certain portion of your audio track. To do this, you'll need to select a portion of the track. To select a portion of your track:

1. On the **Tools** toolbar, click on the **Select** tool.

2. Next, place the mouse pointer on the audio track where you wish to start selecting (where the audio waves are displayed).

3. Click-and-drag the cursor across the track, highlighting the portion that you want to select. The "selected" portion of the audio track will appear in a darker shade of gray.

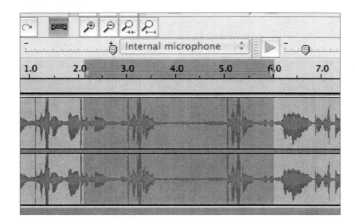

Magnifying your view

By default, when you record audio, the track is displayed in one second intervals. However, you can magnify or zoom in to particular parts of the audio track to identify noises, or to remove or add additional pauses. This magnified view can also give you a clear view of the actual voice waves that were recorded.

To zoom in and out on the audio track:

1. On the **Tools** toolbar, click on the **Zoom In** tool, as seen in the next screenshot.

2. The track will immediately zoom in to show smaller time increments, and more detail of the voice wave.
3. If you want to see even more detail, click on the **Zoom In** tool until you are at the desired level of magnification.
4. To zoom out, click on the **Zoom Out** tool, on the **Tools** toolbar.

5. Again, the track will immediately zoom out in intervals of half a second, to show less detail of your voice waves.

If, for example, you were recording your podcast and a dog barked in the background, you may want to zoom in very closely and *only* see that portion of your audio track in greater detail to try to remove that background noise. You can do this "super" magnification using the following steps:

1. On the **Tools** toolbar, click on the **Select** tool.

2. Select the portion of the audio track where you want to zoom in.

3. When selected, on the main menu click on **View** and then **Zoom to Selection**.

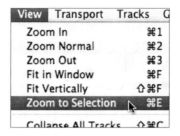

4. The project view will adjust immediately to show only the area that you selected.

Viewing your project

If you recorded more than a few seconds of audio in your sample podcast project (which you probably did), it is likely that your audio track can't be displayed entirely within your Audacity window.

Fit in Window

To display the entire duration of your audio track within the Audacity window, on the main window, select **View,** and then select **Fit in Window**.

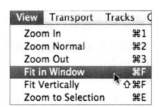

The **Fit in Window** setting displays the entire horizontal timeline for all of the tracks in your project. This means that you won't have to scroll horizontally in the window any more. However, your timeline increments will be much larger and less detailed, especially if you have a really long recording.

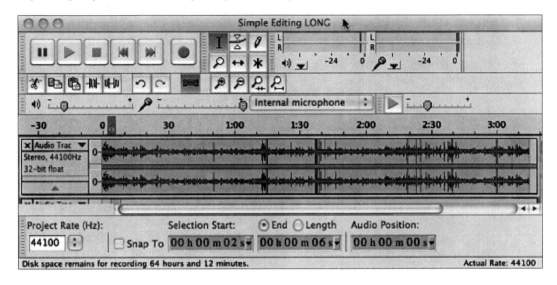

 Ever want to apply this setting quickly? You can use a keyboard shortcut! On a Mac, use *Command + F.* On a PC, use *Ctrl + F.*

Fit Vertically

Beyond our sample project, you may find yourself working with multiple audio tracks. This would require you to scroll up and down to see all of the tracks on the screen. To avoid this inconvenience, on the main window, select **View,** and then select **Fit Vertically**.

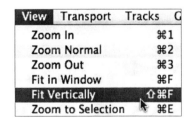

All of the tracks that you are working with will then be displayed from top to bottom in your window, as seen in the next screenshot:

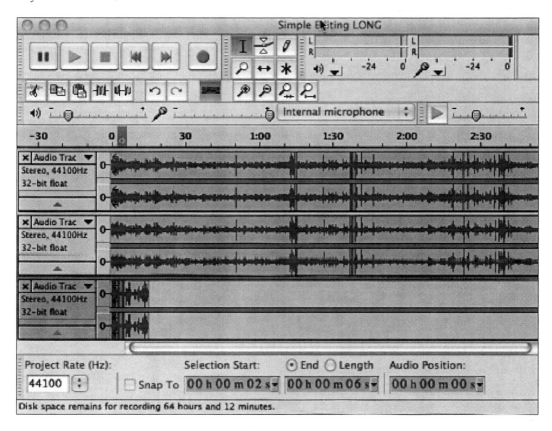

 Ever want to make this setting quickly? On a Mac, use *Up* + *Command* + *F*. On a PC, use *Up* + *Ctrl* + *F*.

The basics of editing

The basic editing features of Audacity include cut, copy, paste, trim, delete, and silence portions of the audio track, all of which can be found in the **Edit** menu on the main menu bar.

They are also available directly from the **Edit** toolbar.

Generally, here's what each of these terms mean:

- To **Undo** an effect or change to the audio track means that you will revert to the previous state of the audio track—in essence, undoing the action you just did.

- When a portion of the audio track is **Cut**, it's removed from the track and is temporarily placed on the computer's clipboard. This clip is still available, in case you want to "paste" into a new track or project (unless you cut or copy another portion - the clipboard can only hold one clip at a time).

- If you **Copy** a portion of the audio track, you are literally making a copy of that selection and placing it on the computer's clipboard for "pasting" into a new track or a new project.

- **Paste** let's you take whatever audio track selection is on the computer's clipboard and place it into a new track or a new project.

- If you **Trim** an audio track, you will remove all audio before and after the selection.

- When you **Delete** a portion of the audio track, you will remove it completely from the track. You can also use the *Delete* key on your keyboard to do the same.

- To **Silence** means that the selected audio is replaced with silence.

Now let's actually edit your audio track to try some of these features.

Cut and Paste

If your podcast ran long—maybe enough for two podcasts—you may want to cut anything past the 3 minute mark and use it to create an additional podcast on your web site. To do this, cut and create another project, as follows:

1. On the **Tools** toolbar, click on the **Select** tool.

2. Starting from the 3:00 minute mark, highlight the audio track until the end of the timeline.

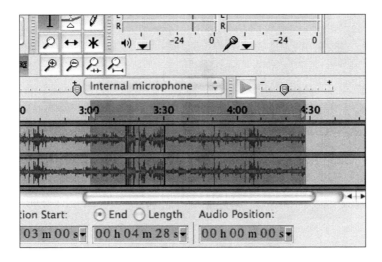

3. From the main menu, click on **Edit,** and then **Cut**.

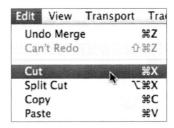

4. The selected piece of audio is "cut" from the timeline (as seen in the next screenshot) and is saved to the computer clipboard.

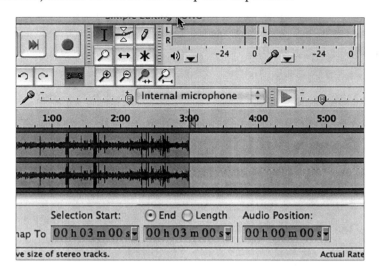

 Suppose you just cut a piece of the voice track and then changed your mind about it. Does the track sound odd? No worries, you can always "undo" the cut by clicking on **Edit** on the main menu, and then selecting **Undo Cut**.

5. To start a new project with the portion of the audio that you just cut, go to the main menu and select **File**, then **New**. A new Audacity window is displayed.

6. From the main menu, select **Edit** and then **Paste**. The cut audio is pasted into this new project.

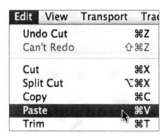

7. To save this new project, select **File** and then **Save Project As**. The start of your new podcast is ready to go! Similarly, if you didn't want to create an entirely new project, you could add the cut portion of the audio as an additional track in your current project. Instead of opening a new project, you would go to the main menu and click on **Edit** and then **Paste**. The cut audio will be added to the current project as an additional track.

Want to play back your newly-edited audio track to make sure that you didn't cut off any of the conversation? Place the cursor near the end of your track, just before your cut, and then click on the **Play** button.

After each major edit, it is important to save your changes, so that you don't lose any of your hard work. From the main menu, click on **File** and then **Save**.

One thing to note when cutting pieces of an audio track: that portion of audio will remain on the clipboard for "pasting" until you perform an additional cut or copy from another portion of the track. If you close Audacity at any time, the content of the clipboard will be lost.

Copy and Paste

A copy is performed much like when you copy a piece of text. The biggest difference is that a copy does not take that portion of the audio "out" of the original audio track. You can use the copy function to duplicate a sound over and over in a track — for example, for comedic effect, or to create your own sound effect. To copy a portion of your audio track and repeat it later in your timeline, use the following steps:

1. Find a sound or word that you'd like to repeat at the end of your podcast.
2. On the **Tools** toolbar, click on the **Select** tool.
3. Highlight the word or sound that you'll be repeating.
4. From the main menu, click on **Edit,** and then **Copy**.

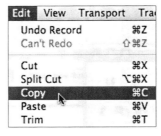

5. Your copied piece of audio is saved to the computer's clipboard.
6. Move to the end of your audio track timeline, and place your cursor at the very end of the recorded audio.

7. Next, from the main menu, select **Edit** then and **Paste**. The cut audio is pasted into the current timeline.

8. For this example, we copied the audio to the very end of the timeline, but you could also paste this clip in at any point in your track, for example, in the middle, or even at the very start.

 Again, even when pasting in additions to your voice track, if it sounds odd, you can always "undo" your previous action. Just go to the main menu, and then select **Edit**, and choose **Undo**.

The intent of this exercise was just practice, but if you want to save the project thus far, to show off everything that you have learned, then from the main menu, click on **File** and then **Save**, to save your work.

Trimming

Trimming an audio selection is very much like cropping a photo using image editing software. You actually crop out the portion of the photo that you want to keep. In audio, it is the same thing — you are removing pieces of audio from before and after the selected portion of the audio track.

1. On the **Tools** toolbar, click on the **Select** tool.

2. Select the portion of your audio track that you wish to keep. Keep in mind that when you trim, the portions of the audio track *not* selected will be deleted.

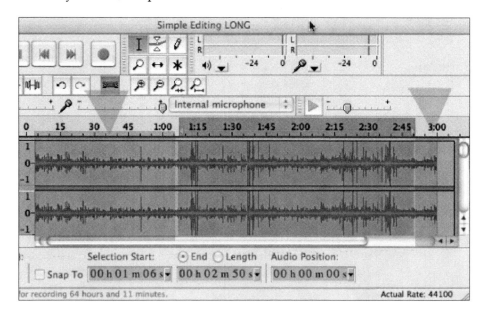

3. From the main menu, click on **Edit** and then **Trim**.

4. The portions of the audio track outside of the selected area will be deleted, as seen in the next screenshot.

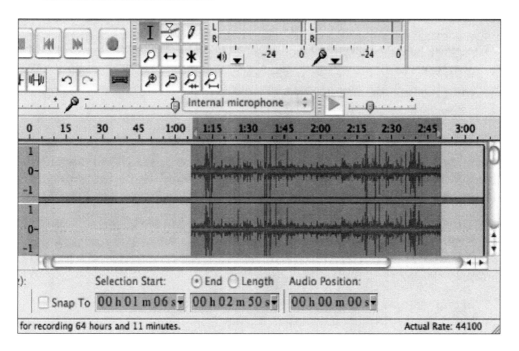

5. Again, if you want to retain this change, save your project (click on **File**, and then select **Save**). If not, you can always undo the trim (click on **Edit**, and then select **Undo Trim**).

 There's a shortcut for performing a trim. After you select the audio that you want to keep, On a Mac, use *Command + T*, or on a PC, use *Ctrl + T*.

Deleting

When recording live audio, there will always be interruptions, long pauses, or sounds that you don't want anyone to hear. These are easy to remedy — you just delete them entirely from the audio track timeline.

1. In your sample recording, find a long pause that you wish to delete (or any unwanted sound). Make a note of where it is in the timeline.

2. On the **Tools** toolbar, click on the **Select** tool.

3. Highlight the sound that you wish to delete, in the timeline.

4. Use the *Delete* key on your keyboard, or on the main menu, click on **Edit** and then **Delete**.

5. Move your cursor to a location just before your deleted portion of the audio track, and click on the **Play** button.

6. Listen to your track and make sure that it sounds as you expect. If not, you can always "undo" your delete. To do this, go to the main menu, click on **Edit**, and then **Undo Delete.** You can try the deletion again, until you get it right.

7. Once it is perfect, save your project again (click on **File** and then **Save**).

Silencing

Like deleting, silencing let's you take out noise, only you aren't actually deleting anything from the timeline, you are just silencing the noise. This is commonly used to take out any background noise (like that barking dog) when no one is speaking.

For example, if you look at your entire audio track, do you see groups of blue lines when you are speaking, and then areas where the audio waves are almost flat, like a moment of silence? You can actually make these moments silences by using this feature.

1. In your sample recording, find a portion that you want silenced. Make a note of where it is in the timeline.

2. On the **Tools** toolbar, click on the **Select** tool.

3. Select the portion of the audio track that you want to silence.

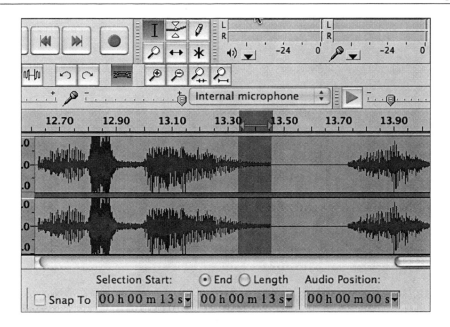

4. On the main menu, click on **Edit** and then **Silence Audio**.

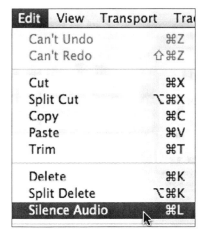

5. The sound that was selected is now visibly flat in the audio track.

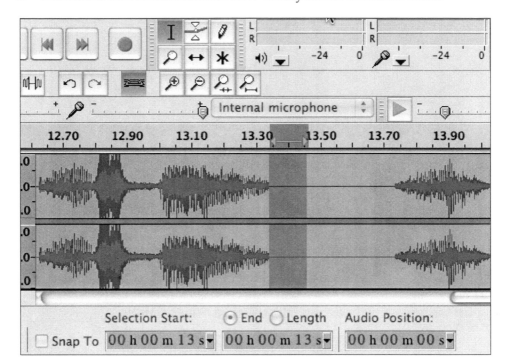

6. Move your cursor to a location just before your newly-silenced portion of the audio track, and then click on the **Play** button.

7. Listen and make sure that your track sounds as you expect. If not, you can always "undo" your silence. To do this, simply go to the main menu, click on **Edit** and then **Undo Silence**, and try it again until you get it right.

8. Once the periods of silence are right where you want them to be, save your project again (click on **File** and then **Save**) to save your changes.

Adjusting volume levels

When we speak, the volume of our voice is never uniform. If you are podcasting phone interviews, you're not always going to get the same volume from the interviewee as your own voice. Audacity allows you to refine your recordings and clarify them to make the sound even. You just need to adjust the volume levels.

The basics are simple—turning up volume levels on a selected piece of an audio track means that you are amplifying it. Turning down the volume levels quite simply means that you are reducing the amplitude of the audio waves. Use the following steps to do this to portions of your audio track:

1. In your sample recording, find an area where the volume is unusually low (maybe because you turned away from the microphone for a moment), or where you want to amplify the output. You can listen to the recording a few times to find such areas, or have a look at your timeline and identify waves with a lesser deviation from the flatline (any area where the voice waves aren't as "high" as the others). Make a note of where the area is in the timeline.

2. On the **Tools** toolbar, click on the **Select** tool.

3. Select the portion of the audio track that you wish to amplify, as seen in the next screenshot:

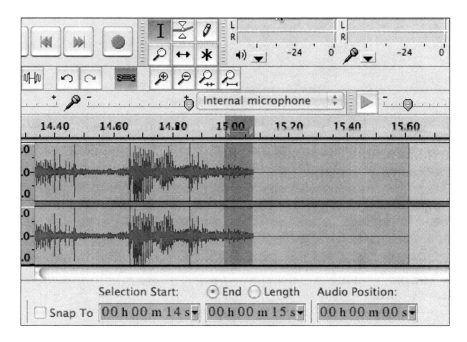

4. On the main menu, click on **Effect** and then **Amplify**. The **Amplify** window is displayed.

5. An example of the **Amplify** window is shown in the next screenshot, and is pretty self explanatory:

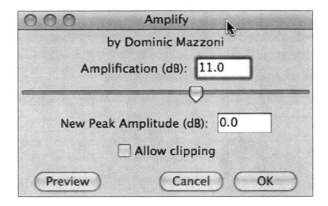

6. If you want to amplify the volume of the selected audio, move the slider to the right-hand side (to a higher positive decibel level). Your ear can hear any differentiation in volume of about 6 dB. To start with, use increments of 6 dB when adjusting this setting. The higher the **Amplification**, the louder the volume. If you decide you want to reduce the volume of this section (lower the decibel level), then move the slider to the left-hand side (negative **Amplification**). Keep in mind that the "higher" the negative number, the lower the volume. To test sound levels, move the slider to the right-hand side by about six additional decibels.

7. Next, click on **Preview**. You'll hear your selected audio at the new decibel or volume level, and can determine if you want to make it even louder or want to keep this new level.

> If you select the **Allow clipping** checkbox, you can amplify the selected audio beyond the highest or loudest audio range recorded for this track. This can cause some distortion in the audio, particularly when your audio has higher sound levels. If you wish to limit these distortions, don't select this checkbox.

8. Click on **OK** when you think you've got it right. You can always listen and make sure that your change sounds as you expect within the audio track. If it does not, you can "undo" it by going to the main menu, and clicking on **Edit** and then **Undo Amplify)**.

9. Once again, if you want to retain these changes, save your project (click on **File** and then **Save**).

Summary

This was your first step into editing with Audacity. We dissected digital voice waves, learned how to navigate in the timeline, and use basic functions in Audacity, such as playback, rewinding, fast forwarding, selecting portions of the voice track, and setting up your Audacity screen to display your entire project on the screen.

You even cut, copied, pasted, trimmed, deleted, adjusted volume levels, and silenced portions of audio in your sample project. These are the the basics that you can apply to almost any audio editing that needs to be done after a recording session.

5
Advanced Editing: Fixing the Glitches and Removing the Noise

What we covered in the previous chapter were the basic editing features of Audacity. In this chapter we are going to get into some more advanced editing options. We are going to use some filters, clean up background noises, use the equalizer, learn how to change some other sound options such as pitch, speed, and tempo and as well as how to normalize volumes and even out the sound across the entire audio track.

Using filters

In audio editing, there are two types of filters: generator and processing. Generator effects artificially create sounds using your audio track (or add it in). Processing effects work with the existing audio and change it to suit your needs. When you install Audacity, there are filters of both types that are already installed. You can also download additional filters, are called plug-ins, that allow you to do even more audio filtering. First, let's discuss a bit more about what filters are and how they can help you when editing audio tracks.

Additional filter plug-ins

There are four types of effects, namely:

- **Internal**—These are the effects that are pre-installed when you install Audacity.

- **Virtual Studio Technology (VST) Plug-ins**—These are what we call third-partly plug ins. They are not bundled with Audacity. You need to add these in after your initial Audacity installation. VST Plug-ins are for Windows or Macintosh computers only.

- **Nyquist Plug-ins**—These are based on the Lisp programming language for sound synthesis and analysis. These are also installed as a plug-in to Audacity after the initial installation. What is unique about them is that anyone can write a Nyquist plug-in for use in a Audacity. All you need is a text editor.

- **Linux Audio Developers Simple Plug-in API (LADSPA)**—These are for Linux users and, just like the VST Plug-ins, don't come in the standard Audacity installation. These need to be installed after you install Audacity.

Plug-in installation

Plug-in installation isn't a difficult process. Generally, you will download a file and then put that file within the `Plug-Ins` folder found inside the `Audacity` folder on your computer. Here's the detailed steps:

1. The plug-in files that you want to add in to Audacity are available at `http://audacity.sourceforge.net/download/plugins`. To download the plug-in files that you need, simply click on the relevant hyperlink. The download will start automatically.

2. Once downloaded, move the compressed file to the `Plug-Ins` folder within the `Audacity` install folder.

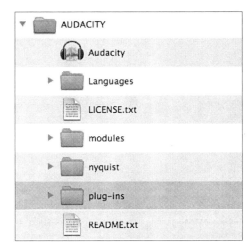

 In the Windows operating system, you can usually find the Audacity folder under Program Files. In Mac OS X, it is under Applications. For Linux, there are multiple distributions available, but a typical location would be within this file path: /usr/share/audacity/plug-ins/.

3. First, take a look at the downloaded files. If the plug-in file is compressed (a ZIP, SIT or DMG file), you may have to double-click on it to uncompress the plug-in files within that folder.

 Read any files marked as README or INSTALL. These typically are installation instructions for that particular plugin.

4. Next, close and restart Audacity. You should then be able to see the new plug-in options in the main menu, under **Effect**, **Generate** or **Analyze** menus.

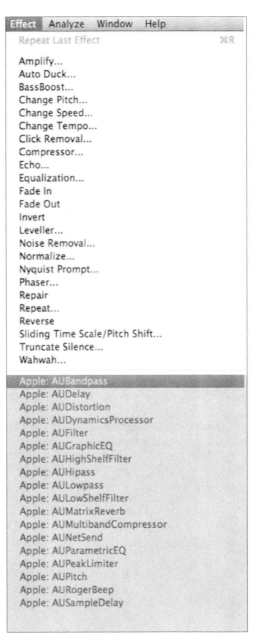

Once the plug-ins have been installed, no matter what the filter type is, you use them all the same way—by going to the main menu and selecting the **Effects**, and then clicking on the desired plug-in or effect. We'll start by using the noise remover filter which is an internal, automatically-installed filter in Audacity.

Removing noise

Noise in audio editing refers to hisses and hums heard on your audio track—not interruptions like a dog barking, or an unwanted voice or word. An example of when we want to use the noise remover filter is where we want to reduce a hissing sound that you can hear throughout your entire recording.

Noise removal as a whole can be very complicated to explain. But in very simple terms, this filter analyzes your audio track after you tell it what you consider "noise" in comparison to all the other sounds. If the "noise" is "heard" the filter silences it in the track without affecting any other sounds. Thus, as implied, noise removal is a two-step process. Let's learn how to do it.

Setting up the noise profile

Setting up the noise profile is the first of two steps for removing noise from your audio track sample project. In this step, you tell Audacity what to consider as noise. We'll do that by selecting a portion of the audio that is silent except for the noise. This can be at the very start of the track, or end of the track. Or, you can magnify the track to find a portion that will help Audacity learn what the noise sounds like. So, let's do that!

1. Open your Audacity sample project.

2. You'll need to find a section of the audio file where there is noise and only noise. So, make sure that you are viewing the track at an interval that let's you visually see something similar to a flat line, but that has small variations that could be attributed to this extra noise. This works best if you have several seconds of this noise (at the beginning or end of a track), but you can select in at any point in your sample track.

Another trick is to record silence for this track and use that as the noise profile. It's as easy as recording about 10 seconds of noise (click on **Record**, wait 10 seconds, then click on **Stop**). Then perform the above step and use this "new" track as the noise profile. Using this method can give you a bit more flexibility by recording many different "noise" profiles based on your recording setup and which track you are editing.

3. Click on the **Select** tool, and select that portion of the track, in order to teach Audacity what is considered quiet.

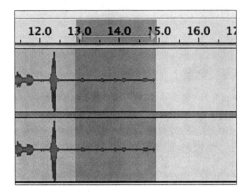

4. Next, on the main menu, click on **Effect** and then **Noise Removal**.

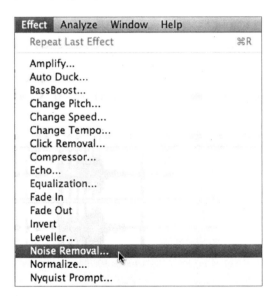

The **Noise Removal** screen is displayed.

5. Click on the **Get Noise Profile** button. Depending on the size of the sample that you selected, this can take anywhere from one to a few seconds. When the window disappears, you are ready to move to the next part of the process.

You've now set your noise profile, and are ready for part two of noise removal.

Removing the noise

Now we are ready to actually analyze the entire audio track and get rid of the noise.

1. In the same project where you just set the noise profile, select a portion, or the entire audio track, in order to start removing the noise. For this example, we will select the entire track by clicking and dragging across the entire timeline, or by using the key combination *Command + A* (or in Windows *Ctrl + A*) on your keyboard.

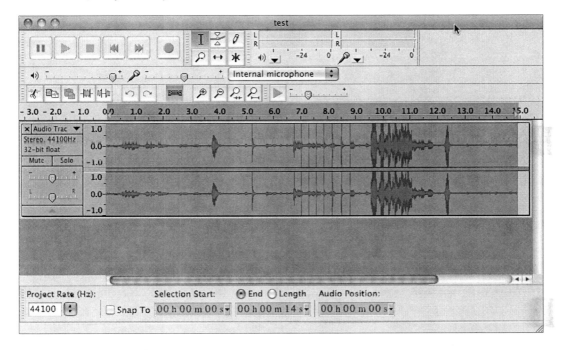

2. Next, on the main menu, click on **Effect**, and then select **Noise Removal** again.

3. You'll see the **Noise Removal** screen again. This time, look at the **Noise reduction** slider, as seen in the next screenshot.

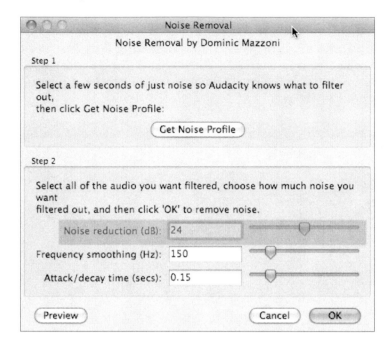

You can move the slider to the left-hand side (for less) or the right-hand side (for more), depending on how much noise you want to remove.

4. Ready to hear a preview? Next, click on the **Preview** button to hear how the current settings would change the audio. If it isn't to your liking, then re-adjust the slider, and click on **Preview** again.

Hearing an Echo?

Moving the **Noise reduction** slider too far to the right-hand side can give you an echo in place of the noise. Essentially, the echo replaces the noise that you're trying to eliminate. Hence, moving the slider to a position at the immediate left of the center will work best.

5. When you like what you hear in the preview, click on **OK**. Once again, depending on the length of your entire audio track, this could take a few seconds to several minutes.

6. Again, because the preview is a very short test, play the entire file to make sure it sounds the way you like. Click on the **Play** button and listen.

7. If for any reason, you don't like what you hear after using the **Noise Removal** effect, you can undo your changes by clicking on **Edit** on the main menu, and then selecting **Undo Noise Removal**.

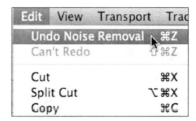

8. If you are satisfied with the noise removal results, save the project so that all of your changes are retained. On the main menu, click on **File,** and then select **Save Project**.

You don't have carry out noise removal for the entire audio track. You can remove noise from selected portions of the track, as well. Just highlight the portions with noise, and perform the previously-described steps. If you select the entire track, it is possible that noise removal will take some of the other sounds away with the noise, and introduce some additional unwanted sounds in the remaining audio. This happens because your noise profile sample might not be applicable throughout the entire audio track, or because the adjustments just aren't as "specific" to each instance of noise removal, consequently causing a bit of distortion in the sound at lower levels in the recording.

Evening out the sound

Don't you just hate it when a commercial suddenly interrupts your favorite television show, especially when its volume is twice as loud as the show you were just watching? Well, in audio recordings, the same thing can happen. If you're interviewing someone on the phone through Skype, or turn your head just slightly and continue talking, there can be significant variations in your volume levels, and consequently your audio will have different volume levels. But this is fixable. You can use the Audacity Compressor utility to make your volume more uniform across the entire track.

The compressor tool lowers the volume of the louder portions of the audio track, and leaves the softer parts alone. This process is called **dynamic range compression**.

Using Compressor

Compressor is an internal effect that is bundled with Audacity. It is just as easy to use as the other effects. Use the following steps to even out the sound levels in your recordings:

1. Open your Audacity sample project.

2. Use the **Selection Tool**, and highlight the section of the audio track that needs its volume levels to be evened out.

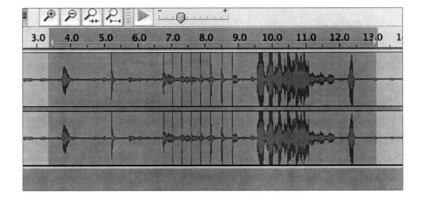

3. Next, in the main menu, click on **Effect**, and then select **Compressor**. The **Compressor** window is displayed.

4. To start with, we'll focus on the setting the **Threshold** — or the maximum volume we want for the entire audio track. Once the threshold is set, any part of the audio that is louder than the this threshold will have its volume reduced. The best practice here is to set the threshold somewhere between the loudest and softest parts of your audio. How do you know your loudest and softest decibel levels? To start with, you can close the **Compressor** window for now. And get ready to take some notes. First, set your **Output level meter** to dB (decibels). **Decibels** is a unit of measurement used to describe the intensity, or loudness, of a sound. To make this setting, click on the small arrow to the right of the **Output level meter**.

5. Select **dB** from the drop-down menu.

6. Click on the **Play** button to listen to your selection, but this time, pay close attention to the **Output level meter** bar.

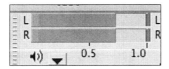

7. Pay attention to the left-hand side of the level meter with green bars. This is the **Output level meter**, and it is a visual representation of the volume level of the playback. Since we just changed the measurement to decibels, we will also see the specific volume levels below the green bars. You'll notice different shades of green on the output level meter bars. The light green of the bar indicates the average volume level, and the dark green indicates the highest volume level.

8. Look for of the loudest portions of your track (the dark green) and mark that dB level. Then take note of the softest portions of when you speak, and mark down that dB level which will (will be below the average volume level shown in light green). As an example, if the loudest part is -2 dB and the softest is -20 dB, then you should set a threshold of -12 dB—which is approximately half way between the two.

9. Now go back to the main menu, click on **Effects**, and then select **Compressor**. Next, slide the threshold slider by clicking and dragging it to your determined threshold level. In the previous example, we'd set the threshold to -12 dB.

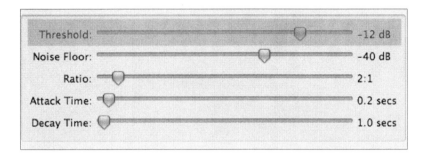

10. The next setting to adjust is **Ratio**, which sets the level of compression. Typically the default setting of 2:1 works well. But you can adjust it to sync with other settings. The higher the first number, the more compression (volume adjusting) that is performed.

11. You can also leave the **Attack Time** setting as its defaults. This setting tells Audacity how fast to apply your compression ratio. A setting of 0.2 generally works best.

12. Again, we will leave the **Make-up gain for 0dB after compressing** check box selected. **Gain** is the level of amplification or increased volume given to an audio track. Leaving this check box selected is important because it forces an overall increase in the volume of the recording in its entirety.

13. When you're all set, click on the **Preview** button to hear what your audio track will sound like.

14. If you like the result, click on **OK** to complete the compression process. This could take a couple of seconds or a few minutes, depending on how large a selection you chose to adjust.

As with all other editing that we do, make sure that you play the entire audio track again to make sure that the settings are to your liking. Click on the **Skip to Start** button, and then click on **Play**.

 Don't like it? You can undo your edits by using *Command + Z* on a Mac (or *Ctrl + Z* in Windows) to undo compression. You can also click on **Edit** in the main menu, and then select **Undo Compression**.

If you like it, save the project by going to the main menu, and then selecting **File** and **Save Project**.

Normalizing

This is a great setting if you just want to make all of your audio tracks (in our example we are only using one track, but you can add more!) as loud as possible. Basically, you are forcing them all to be at the same volume level, and as loud as they can be. Use the following steps to set this up:

1. Open your project.

2. Go to the main menu and click on **Effect**, and then select **Normalize**.

3. Use the defaults on this screen, and then click on **OK**.

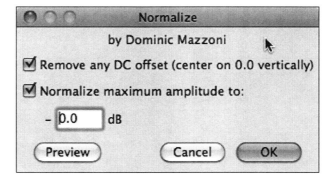

4. If you are satisfied with the noise removal results, save the project so that all of your changes are saved. From the main menu, select **File** and then **Save Project**.

This is a safe effect, in that it will never make your sample so loud as to introduce distortion. This is one of the easiest ways to increase your volume, but it is equally important that you watch out for over-compression—specifically with music tracks. It is okay that your audio track has areas where the sound is quiet and then loud with distinct differences between them. This gives a richer listening experience.

More sound effects

Because we are discussing the ways in which we can manipulate sound, here's a few others that you can change in your test project, if you see fit:

Changing pitch

Changing the pitch in audio editing means changing the high or low tone that we hear in the track. Technically, this means that we are decreasing the time interval between the voice waves (which means that we are increasing frequency). In theory, if you do this, it will also increase the speed or tempo of the entire track. But with Audacity, you can change this pitch setting without changing the speed of your audio track because Audacity will re-adjust to maintain the original speed.

To change the pitch, follow the steps shown below:

1. Open up your test project, and select the portion you want to change the pitch (or select the entire track).

2. From the main menu, click on **Effect** and then **Change Pitch**. The **Change Pitch** window is displayed.

3. Use the slider bar along the bottom of the screen, and move it to the left-hand side to lower the pitch, or to the right-hand side to make the pitch higher.

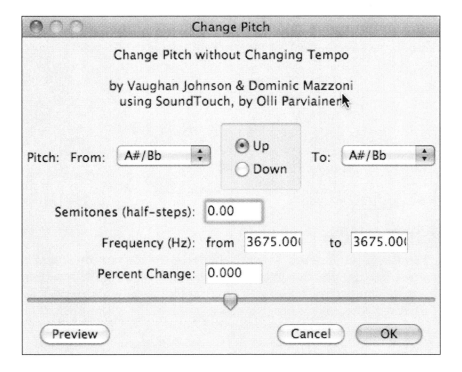

4. Again, you can preview your changes by clicking on the **Preview** button.

5. Click on **OK** when you are satisfied with the setting, and the pitch of your selection will be changed.

6. If you are satisfied with the noise removal results, save the project so that your work is saved. From the main menu, click on **File,** and then select **Save Project**.

 Don't like it? You can undo your edits by using *Command + Z* on a Mac (or *Ctrl + Z* in Windows) on your keyboard.

Changing the speed

If you really do want to change the speed of you audio track, there is a way to do that, too. However, this will also change the pitch *and* shorten your overall track length, because you are literally making the audio track, in essence, play faster.

To change the speed of your audio track, use the following steps:

1. Open up your test project, and select the portion for which you want to change the speed of playback.

2. From the main menu, click on **Effect,** and then select **Change Speed.** The **Change Speed** window is displayed.

3. Again, the easiest way to change this setting to your liking is to adjust the slider bar. Move it to the left-hand side to slow down the speed, or to the right-hand side to make it faster.

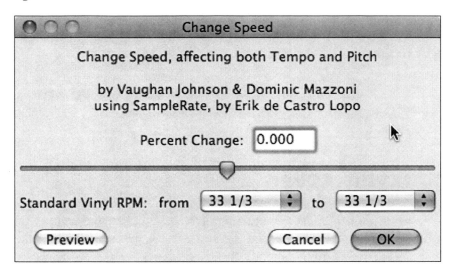

4. Again, you can preview your changes by clicking on the **Preview** button.

5. Click on **OK** when you are satisfied with the setting, and the pitch of our selection will be changed.

6. If you are satisfied with the noise removal results, save the project so that your changes are retained. From the main menu, click on **File,** and then select **Save Project**.

 Don't like it? You can undo your edits by using *Command* + *Z* on a Mac (or *CTRL* + *Z* in Windows) on your keyboard.

Changing the tempo

Changing the speed (and pitch) isn't always what you need, either. What if you need to increase the speed of one portion of the audio track, but don't want to change the pitch of anyone's voice? In this case, you change the **Tempo** in Audacity. Tempo is the speed or pace of a piece of audio when it is played.

Here's the simple steps to do this:

1. Open up your test project, and select the portion for which you want to change the tempo.

2. From the main menu, click on **Effect**, and then select **Change Tempo**. The **Change Tempo** window is displayed.

3. As with the other sound effects described in this section, the slider bar is the easiest and fastest way to change this setting. Move it to the left-hand side to slow down the tempo, and to the right-hand side to make it faster.

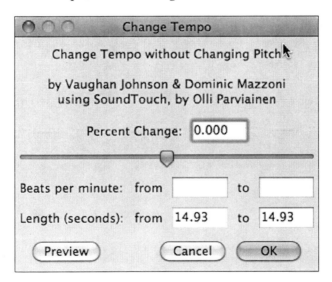

4. Again, you can preview your changes by clicking on the **Preview** button.

5. Click on **OK** when you are satisfied with the setting, and the pitch of our selection will be changed.

6. If you are satisfied with the noise removal results, save the project so that all of your changes are retained. From the main menu, click on **File**, and then select **Save Project**.

 Don't like it? You can undo your edits by using *Command* + *Z* on a Mac (or *Ctrl* + *Z* in Windows) on your keyboard. You can also click on the **Edit** menu and select **Undo Change Tempo**.

Summary

We spent a lot of time in this chapter manipulating the sound in our audio track. We learned about the different types of filters, how to install additional effects, and how to use the noise removal feature. We also learned about the equalizer, and about changing pitch, speed, and tempo. We even learned how to even out volumes within a track. With these basics, it's likely that your sample project is ready to be exported into the final podcast format, so that's what we are going to learn next.

6
Saving Projects and Exporting Podcasts

We've spent the last few chapters learning how to record an audio track and then edit it by using some basic editing features, how to get rid of "noise", and even spent some time talking about how to silence or delete pieces of unwanted audio. Now it is time to learn how to save your project in its final state and export it in different audio file formats so that you can send it out as a final podcast, or post it on a website for download. We'll even discuss how to use ID3 tags for your podcast (artist, genre, title, and so on), the best tips and tricks for compressing your final projects into a decent file size, and preparations for uploading it to a web hosting service.

Audio formats to which Audacity exports

We discussed in the first chapter how Audacity can save files in many file formats. When you save a project, it is saved as an AUP, or **Audacity Project**, file with a corresponding folder with the same name as the project, which contains all of the additional project files. But when you export a file, everything is converted and then saved into one file. Export file formats supported by Audacity without additional software are:

- AIFF (Apple) signed 16 bit PCM
- WAV (Windows) signed 16 bit PCM
- GSM 6.10 WAV (mobile)
- Ogg Vorbis files
- FLAC files
- MP2 files

Additional export formats are available by installing simple plug-ins or libraries that add additional functionality to Audacity. These formats, and their associated plug-ins, are:

- MP3, with the LAME MP3 encoding library
- Various FFmpeg formats, such as, M4A (AAC), and WMA, are supported through the FFmpeg import or export library
- Various other uncompressed file formats, such as: AU, AVR, HTK, IFF, and so on

Podcast formats

Podcasts can be in any number of audio formats—as long as someone can listen to it on their computer or handheld audio device. But, by far, the most common podcast format is MP3. This is a compressed file format. Compressed formats mean that the quality of the recorded audio is lowered in order to make the file size smaller, but the lost quality won't be noticeable by most people. Also, in this case, it exports an audio file into a single file that is easy to share with others. We'll learn how to export in MP3 format, and discuss other formats that might be useful.

The term—or audio file extension—MP3 is short for MPEG-1 Audio Layer 3. At a very high level this is an audio compression standard used when exporting audio. The file sizes are small, and it is easy to send these files through e-mail, or post them on an Internet site for someone to download.

Compression means that all of the audio is combined and exported to a single file. The quality is reduced by using lower bitrates. For example, traditional music found on a CD is recorded at 1411.2 kilobytes per second (kbps) and a high quality MP3 is saved at rates like 320 kbps. But MP3s could be saved as low as 8 kbps, which reduces the file size considerably depending on the sound quality you want.

Installing libraries

Before you jump in and get ready to export your podcast to MP3, you'll need to install a library that allows you to encode (or digitize) MP3 files. Due to software patents, Audacity can't package these libraries with the program itself, so we'll download and install manually.

We're going to use LAME, a high quality MP3 encoder licensed under the General Public License (GPL). This means that it can be widely distributed with open source software projects like Audacity. Installation is easy, in that you just have three basic steps: download, extract, and save the files to the Audacity folder. So let's do that.

1. Open a web browser and go to the LAME download page at
    `http://lame.buanzo.com.ar/`.

 NOTE: This site uses a form of protection called anti-hotlinking. It allows you to download files from it directly, as long as browser configurations and permissions are set to common/usual settings.

2. Find the appropriate LAME file for your computer's operating system, and then click on the link to download the compressed file.

3. Once downloaded, double-click on the `.dmg` (for Mac computers) or `.exe` (for Windows) file to start the installation. For Linux, there are multiple distributions available. Download and install the file, based on that version's installation instructions.

4. You will be prompted to save the library file, which is called: `libmp3lame.dylib`. You can save this anywhere on your computer, but we recommend that you place it in the **Audacity** folder on your computer so that you remember where to find it when prompted when you save your first MP3 file.

 For the Windows operating system, you can usually find the **Audacity** folder in **Program Files**. In Mac OS X, it is in **Applications**.

5. Once you save the **Lame Library** file, you're all set for now.

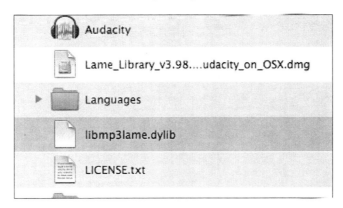

Exporting your project as an MP3

Exporting is the basic process of converting your source project files into the desired file format. Typically, the file format that you want the final files to be in. To do this is pretty simple. You just open your project and export it, then add some tagging information to your file, and finally convert and save the file. Let's get started!

Opening and exporting your project

To get started, just open the Audacity project file that you want to export. In our case, it is the test project that we've been working on since the beginning of this book.

1. Open Audacity, and then choose **File** and then **Open**.

2. Choose your project file, and then click on **Open**. The project opens in the Audacity main window.

You can also always open a recent project by going to the main menu and selecting **File** and then **Open Recent**. Another menu is displayed, showing the last open projects for easy and quick access to re-open them.

3. When you are ready to start the export, you just select **File** and then **Export.**

4. The **Edit Metadata** window is displayed.

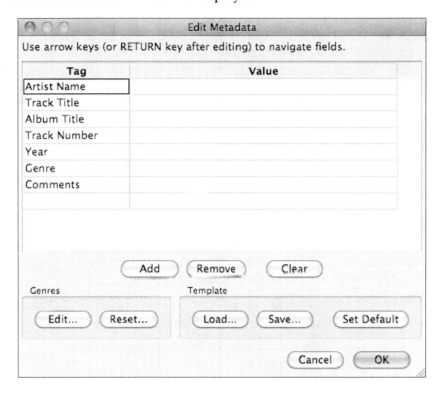

5. You're then ready for the next section, *Adding Tagging Information*.

You don't need to export your entire audio track!

If you have a really long audio track in one project and just want to export a portion of it to an MP3 (say, a two-part interview podcast), you can export a selection instead of the entire audio track. Just select the portion of the audio file you want to export, and then choose **File** and **Export Selection.** Then, continue with *Adding tagging information*.

Adding tagging information

Audio files, no matter what format they are in, can store some tagging or metadata information in the file, in order to make it more "usable" by the end user. Tags, or Metadata, include items such as the artist or creator name, track title, genre, and album title. This information, once tied to the audio file, is used by audio players on your computer, such as Windows Media Player or iTunes. When someone selects this audio file to play it, you can see all of this tagging information. This information can also be useful for sorting or categorizing a large library of audio files.

So, once you choose **Export** from the **File** menu, as you did previously, you can start filling in the information in the **Edit Metadata** window.

To start entering tagging information, follow the steps shown below:

1. Just move you mouse to the **Value** field of any of the **Tag** fields, and click within that row. Then enter the specific information for that file.

2. Select another **Tag Value** and enter the required information, until you have added all of the metadata necessary.

    For example:

    ○   In **Artist Name**, you could enter your name.

    ○   In **Track Title**, enter a title for this track (that is, Test Podcast).

    ○   For **Genre**, when you click on the **input** field, you are offered a drop-down box to choose from a standard list of musical genre options. You can also type in your own special **Genre**.

    ○   The **Comments** field is open. This means that, you can enter any other relevant information that you would like, here. An example might be: *Interview with Audacity Author detailing how to make a Podcast*.

3. You can also add additional **Tags**. Click on the **Add** button on this screen. An additional row is added to the table, which offers empty **Tag** and **Value** fields for you to use however you would like.

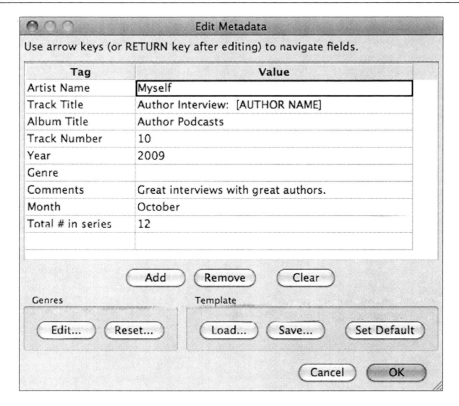

None of the fields in this window are required, but they are useful if completed. Again, it provides information to an end user about what the file contains without actually having to open or play the file.

A couple other helpful areas on this screen are **Genres** and **Templates**. These are explained below.

Genres

The **Genres** section lets you edit the pre-populated drop-down list that is shown when you select the **Genre Value** in the **Metadata** area of the screen.

Here, if you click on **Edit**, you can delete, change, and add the options in the predefined list. Just make sure that you click on **OK** when you are done, to save your additional or modified genres.

 If you are using Linux, this text box is not selected by default, but it is editable. Select it and you can add custom genres as described.

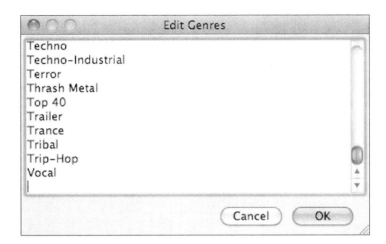

The added custom genres will be kept in the **Genre** list until you perform a reset, even if you close and re-open Audacity.

If you need to reset the list, go back to the **Edit Metadata** screen, click on **Reset**, and any changes that you made to the predefined list will be deleted and the original **Genre** list will be restored.

Templates

Setting up a template for metadata tags can be helpful if you are creating a series of audio tracks that will have similar information.

For example, if you were going to do a series of podcasts interviewing famous authors, the Album Title, Year, Genre, and even parts of a Track Title might be the same. Instead of typing these in over and over and over—you can set up a template that has all of these known fields already populated.

Here's how it's done:

1. Just as you entered tagging data for the single audio track before, you would enter common tags into this screen that you would want to use for every track in your collection.

2. Feel free to add a few tags here that are relevant to you extended project.

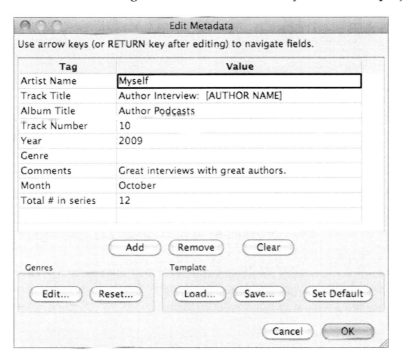

3. When all of the common tags are entered, click on **Save**.

4. Give this **Metadata** or **Tag** template a name, and then click on **Save**.

Now, when you are ready to export your next Author Interview Podcast, you can click on **Load**, select this template and all the fields that you previously set are already populated. Update what you need, to and then continue to save your exported MP3 file.

Saving your exported file

Once the tagging information is in place, you are ready to actually save the file.

1. On the **Edit Metadata** window, once complete, click on **OK**. The **Save As** window is displayed:

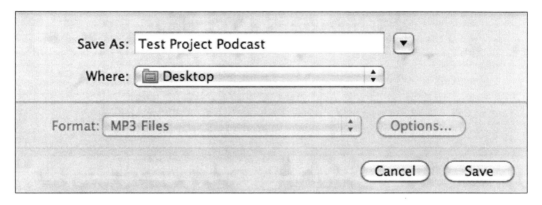

2. Type in a name for the exported file in the **Save As** field. By default, the project name is entered into this field, but you can name the file whatever you like.

3. In the **Where** field, you can choose to where you would like the file to be saved.

4. Lastly, in the **Format** drop down list, select **MP3**. For your future projects, you can choose any of the supported audio formats in this field.

5. Unsure of the exact MP3 settings and want to make sure that they are set correctly? Click on **Options**. The **Specify MP3 Options** window is displayed, as seen in the next screenshot.

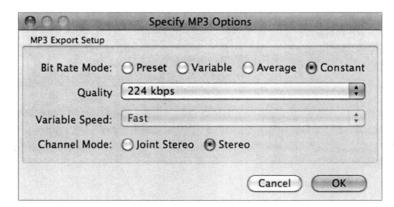

6. Here, you can set the **Bit Rate Mode**, **Quality**, **Variable Speed** and the **Channel Mode**. Here's a quick definition for what each of these variables mean to the MP3 export process:

   ○ **Bit Rate Mode** gives you four options for the quality versus file size setting during this export. If you choose Presets, you can choose between three pre-determined settings recommended by the LAME developers. **Variable Bit Rate Mode** will change the bitrates used based on the complexity of the sound in the audio file. It does this to try to maintain consistent quality of the audio throughout. Selecting **Average Bit Rate Mode** sets a specific bitrate for the track, with some changes based on the sound complexity. This setting won't give as consistently high quality file as the **Variable** bitrate, but gives you more control over the file size. A **Constant** bitrate sets a specific bitrate for the audio file with no fluctuation based on the content of the audio file itself. This setting gives the worst quality output.

   ○ The **Quality** setting lets you choose the exact bitrate (kilobits per second or kbps) to use when encoding your file. The general rule is the higher the bitrate the better the quality, but also the larger the file size.

   ○ **Variable Speed** is only available if you choose the **Variable** bitrate mode. This setting calculates how fast and accurately the encoding process will be performed. **Standard** traditionally gives the best results, but takes longer to complete than the **Fast** option.

   ○ The two options in **Channel Mode** determine how the two channels of a stereo recording are processed during encoding. **Joint Stereo** converts the left and right channels into two different signals. This is best used for recordings that don't have many differences between stereo channels, as it makes encoding more efficient and quicker to perform. **Stereo Channel Mode** encodes each of the channels separately and independently, in order to give the best encoding possible for each.

7. For our project, you can set the **Quality** rate to **224 kbps** and leave the rest as it is. Then click on **OK**.

8. If this is the first time that you have performed an export using Audacity, you will be asked to find the LAME Library that you saved at the beginning of this chapter. Click on **Browse**, and go to the Audacity installation folder to find the `libmp3lame.dylib` file.

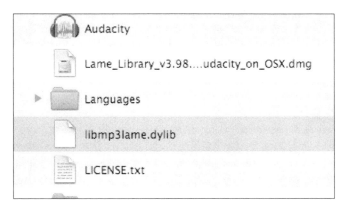

9. Click on **Save**. Your very first MP3 podcast is created and saved!

Want to test it out? Just double-click on the MP3 file that you just saved and you'll be listening to your very first podcast!

Distributing your podcast

There are any number of ways that you can post or offer your podcast to others. The easiest, if your file size is small (under 8 MB), is to just e-mail your audio file to a friend. Or you can store it on a portable USB drive to help transport it to another computer for another person to hear. However, typically you want a larger audience than your neighbor or family, which means that you'll need to find a way to broadcast the podcast or share it through the Internet or a free podcast library. We will outline the details of doing each of these options next.

Sending the file

If all you need to do is share your podcast with a select few (or even have an interviewee approve your podcast for broadcast) you can simply attach the MP3 file to an e-mail message in most mail programs and send the file directly. That is one of the advantages of using the MP3 format—the file sizes are typically small enough for e-mail servers to accept.

Uploading to a website

Often, podcasts are shared on websites or blogs for others to download. All of this however, is dependent on whether you already have a website with a host account (this means that you have files saved on a web server that you can access through an FTP or web-based interface), or have a blog set up with one of the many free blogging services available online (Wordpress, Blogger, or Typepad, to name a few).

Website with hosting

If you already have a website set up and are updating the content regularly, adding a list of podcasts isn't difficult. You just need to:

1. Upload your podcast MP3 file to your host service through FTP or a web interface.

2. Remember where you placed the file on your web server so that you can create a direct link to the file.

3. On the web page where you want people to download or listen to your podcast, create a link to the file that you just uploaded.

Free blogging service

With many of the free blogging services on the web, you can also share your podcasts. Ways to post your audio files will vary with each service that you use, but at a most basic level you will need to:

1. Create a new blog account (if you don't already have one) on any of the blog sites listed above (or others). When you do this, you can choose a blog name, web address (URL), description, and more. If you already have a blog, then just log in to your account.

2. Create a new blog post. Ideally, you would give the blog post a title, and a few sentences to describe your podcast in order to interest anyone who finds your blog.

3. Then you create a link, and upload your audio file to your blog.

 Some blogging services might not let you upload audio files directly to your blog. See your service provider's help center for more details if you can't do this directly from the web interface.

4. When the upload is complete, click on **Publish** to post the new blog entry. Once you've received confirmation that your new post is live, go to your blog URL, and you should be able to view and listen to your podcast.

RSS feeds

Really Simple Syndication (RSS) feeds are a way to continually broadcast (or publish) items such as podcasts and blog entries and sometimes even for videos. You've likely already heard of these for news headlines. These feeds are in a standardized XML format and pull the metadata tags that you assigned when exporting your podcast. These feeds are displayed in "readers" for others to automatically receive. Feed readers allow subscribers (those who choose to receive feeds from your site your site), to receive updates as soon as you post any new information. In this case, this is every time that you release a new podcast.

When using a RSS reader, the user needs to enter the feed's URL or web address to complete a subscription. Then, the RSS reader checks these subscribed feeds URLs regularly for new updates, and then alerts the user when new podcasts are available.

For each of the ways to distribute you podcast above, there are distinct ways to create an RSS feed for your podcast. Here's a few options that you can explore:

- For a website with hosting, where you have posted your podcast, you can create RSS feeds by using a simple RSS feed provider, such as FeedBurner (`www.feedburner.com`). These services are free, and once you provide a link to your website area where you will post podcasts, they do the rest automatically for you. You'll have to set up an account, and then make a note of the Podcast RSS feed URL (it typically ends in `.xml`). Then, on your website, you can offer a link to subscribe to your Podcast RSS feed, through this URL.

- When using a blogging service, there are usually ways to automatically set up RSS feeds to your blog entries. Explore your blogging service provider's site to determine how best to set up RSS feeds for your podcasts.

Uploading to iTunes

Many people use the iTunes software on their computers to subscribe to podcasts to listen to on their computer or iPod. Now that you have a completed podcast, you can submit your work to the iTunes Store, as well.

The iTunes Store has a podcast directory that helps you to find and subscribe to podcasts. There is no fee to add your podcasts to this directory, but you'll need to create a podcast RSS feed, create an iTunes account, and provide a link to the podcast RSS feed that you have already set up. Here's the details:

1. If you haven't already done so, download iTunes from here: http://www.apple.com/itunes/overview/.

2. Install iTunes on your computer.

3. Once installed, make sure that you have your podcast file ready. It has to be in either of the M4A or MP3 format.

4. Place your podcast on your blog or website, and create the RSS feed. See the *RSS feeds* section earlier in this chapter for how to do this.

5. Next, open up iTunes, and then click on **iTunes Store** in the left-hand side panel.

6. Choose **Podcasts** from the iTunes Store navigation panel.

7. Then click on **Submit a Podcast** on the right-hand side of the screen.

8. Now the submission process begins! Enter the URL for your podcast RSS feed, and then click on **Continue**.

9. The iTunes Store reads the metadata tags that you entered when you created the podcasts, and then displays this information on the summary screen. You might also be asked for more information, such as language, category, and whether the podcast requires explicit tags.

10. Lastly, you will have to wait for iTunes approval of your podcast. Once approved, you should be able to search or browse the iTunes podcast directory and find your podcast! And of course, add more episodes later!

 Make sure that all your podcasts are in either AAC (M4A) or MP3 format, because these are the only formats thatthe iTunes store will accept. And, of course, there are rules about copyrighted material (such as music) being included in your podcast, so make sure that you check out more information here: `http://www.apple.com/itunes/podcasts/creatorfaq.html`, before you begin.

Other Export File Options

As stated at the very beginning of this chapter, Audacity allows you to export your audio tracks in many other audio formats besides MP3. Exporting in those other formats is just as easy.

1. From an open project, just select **File** and then **Export**.

2. Just as you did before, enter tagging information in the **Edit Metadata** window, and once completed, click on **OK**.

3. In the **Save** window, type in a name for the exported file.

4. In the **Where** field, you can choose where you would like the file to be saved.

5. This time, in the **Format** drop down, choose your preferred file format.

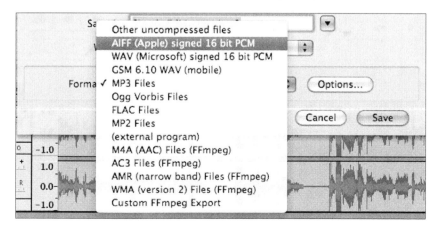

7. Just like before, you can click on **Options** to change any bitrate, speed, or quality settings.

8. Finally, click on **OK**, and your file will be saved in the audio format of your choice.

You can even export more than one audio track at a time!

If you have a project in Audacity that has more than one track in the timeline, you can export each track as a separate file. All you need to do is select **File** and then **Export Multiple** or **Export Labels**.

Summary

In this chapter, we learned how to save your project in its final state, and how to export it in different audio types so that you can send it out as a final podcast, or post it on a website for download. We even discussed how to add some metadata tags for your podcast (artist, genre, title, and so on), and all the details for distributing your podcast, including posting to your own website or blog, and submitting it to the iTunes Store podcast directory. We even discussed in some detail how to export in other formats besides MP3.

Now that we have covered the basics, and even exported a finished podcast, we're going to spend the next chapter going into more advanced Audacity capabilities. We will use more than one audio track, and learn how to split, duplicate, overdub, and a whole bunch more, so that your podcasts can become even better and more professional.

7
Beyond the Basics: Editing for Even Better Sound

In previous chapters we learned the basics of cleaning up voice tracks and removing background noise, but there's a bunch more that we can do. Working with the audio tracks, we can make sounds appear more seamless, soften certain kinds of sounds, such as sibilants, clip and replace sounds, and even time shift, all of which are more advanced editing techniques. Let's take a look at the steps to use each of these techniques, in order to help with any future Audacity projects that you might start.

Softening sibilants

Sibilant sounds are "s", "sh", and "ch" that hiss and seem a bit harsh in comparison to the rest of the audio track. The idea is to soften those specific sounds without ruining the sounds of your other consonants. Some people call this **de-essing**. There are a few effect plug-ins available to help lessen these sounds, such as Spitfish (`http://www.digitalfishphones.com/main.php?item=2&subItem=5`) combined with VST Enabler (`http://audacityteam.org/vst/`). But you can also do this manually in Audacity with just a few steps, which works well for shorter audio track editing.

Want to help minimize sibilant sounds BEFORE you record?

Before hitting the record button, hang your microphone above your head, or have it point slightly at your nose. That way, when you are recording, the sound waves aren't "hitting" the microphone at an angle that might create sibilants. Also, practicing your script a few times can help you sound more natural.

1. Open you Audacity project.

2. Listen to your track and find an area where you hear a high-pitched or strong "S" sound. This is a sibilant that we'll work to soften.

3. Use the **Select Tool** and highlight that sound.

 You might have to zoom into the sound waves to select it exactly. If you are using a mouse and it has a wheel on it, you can use the mouse wheel to magnify or zoom to smaller portions of the timeline as well. Use *Ctrl + Mouse Scroll Up* to zoom in, or *Ctrl + Mouse Scroll Down* to zoom out.

4. From the main menu, select **Effect** and then **Amplify**.

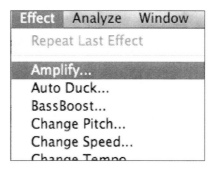

5. In the **Amplify** window, change the **Amplification** field to -2 decibels.

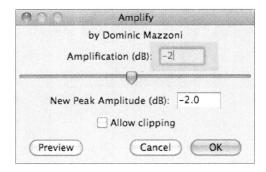

You will see that the level of the audio wave form gets smaller.

6. Play back that section, and see if it sounds better.

7. If not, repeat steps 5 and 6 until you have the desired level for the sibilant.

8. Keep listening, to find more sibilants that you would like to correct. Repeat steps 3 through 7 until you have reached the end of your audio track.

Finally, save your project again (from the main menu, select **File** and then **Save**) to keep the work.

Clip and replace sounds

Clipping and replacing sounds is the process of selecting a sound that you want to replace with another. This can be done quite simply.

First, make sure that you record or import the sound that you want to have added into the original project file.

*   If you just want to re-record that section, then you can do that from your current Audacity project screen by first muting your main audio track (click on **Mute**), clicking on **Record**, and then saying the new words or phrase.

- If you want to import an already-recorded clip, then in your already open Audacity project, go to the main menu and select **File,** and then **Import | Audio**.

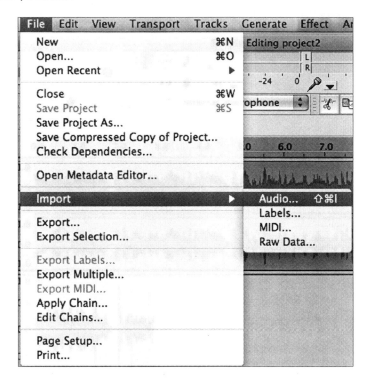

- Select the file that you want to import, and then click on **OK**.

In either of the previous scenarios, you will see that the new track (pre-recorded, or just recorded) will be displayed below the track that is already in your project.

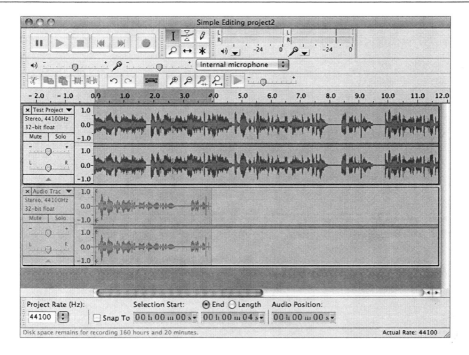

Now, the steps are easy:

1. From the new audio track on your screen, select the words or phrase that you want to be swapped into the original track.

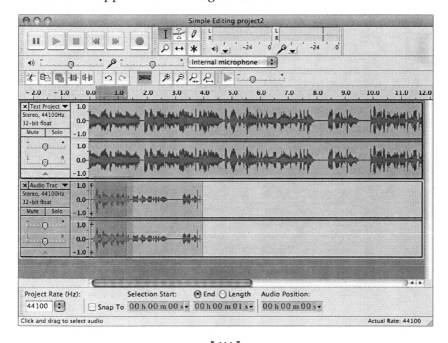

2. On the main menu, select **Edit,** and then **Copy**. That selection is now saved to the virtual clipboard.

3. Now go to your original audio track and select the portion of the audio you want to be replaced.

 Don't worry, you can click, and play, and click and zoom in this audio track to find the exact spot that you want to replace.

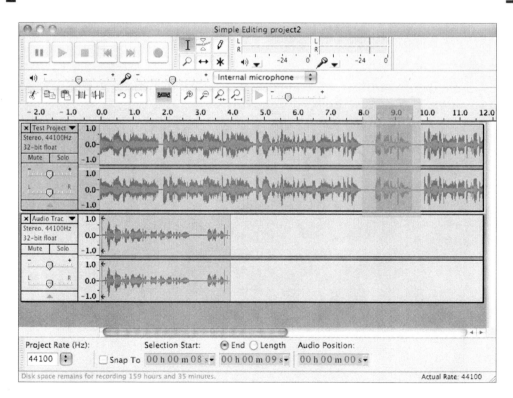

4. When you have the portion that you want replaced selected, from the main menu select **Edit** and then **Paste**.

This will replace the selected material with the contents of the clipboard.

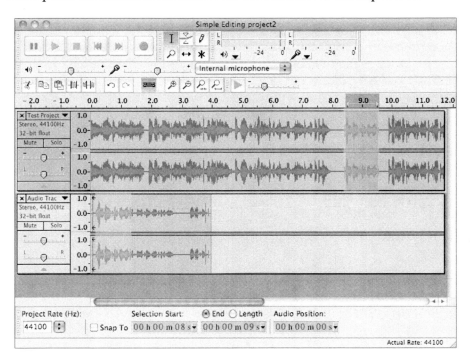

If you are trying to replace phrases or words in the original track and want the new segment to blend more into the original track, the following list offers a few tips:

- In the original track, don't cut or delete the unwanted words or phrases— silence them instead (select **Edit,** and then **Silence Audio**)
- Use a separate track to record the new words or phrases
- Try to re-create the recording environment used for the original recording

- Use the **Time Shift Tool**, as described in the next section, to move this new phrase into the exact spot of the unwanted one that has been silenced

- In all tracks, make sure that as much background noise as possible has been removed

- Work with amplification to make sure that the overall volume level is the same between the original and new phrases

- Using **Fade In** or **Fade Out** and the **Envelope Tool** can help blend the two tracks together

- Always keep any background music as a separate track to any vocal music.

Aligning tracks and using Time Shift

If you are using more than one audio track in your project, you might need to align the tracks so that they start at the same time, move voice tracks so that they start at the correct times, or even move one track to start later than another. To do all of this, the **Time Shift** and **Align** tools can help.

Using Time Shift

The time shift tool is very easy to use. With your Audacity project open, make sure that the audio track that you want to move is highlighted:

1. Select the **Time Shift Tool**.

2. Click-and-drag the track that you want to move to the desired position.

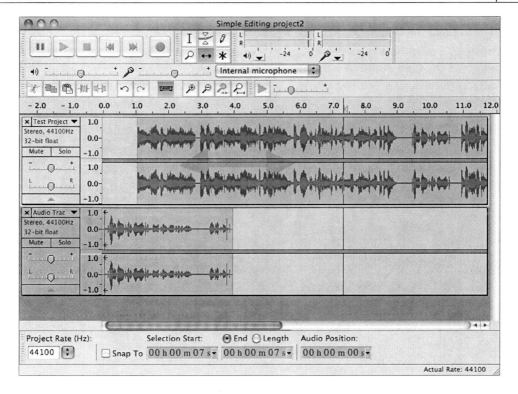

3. Release the mouse button to place the track in this new location.

To make more precise time shifts

Zoom in to the audio track. This is easy to do with shortcut keys. When you have the **Time Shift Tool** selected, you can use *Ctrl + 1* on a Windows computer or *Command + 1* on a Mac. To zoom out, you use *Ctrl + 3* on a Windows computer or *Command + 3* on a Mac. Want to go back to the default magnification? Use *Ctrl + 2* or *Command + 2* respectively.

If you are using a mouse with a wheel, on either operating system, you can use the mouse wheel to zoom in and out of the audio track, as well. Use *Ctrl + Mouse Scroll Up* to zoom in, or *Ctrl + Mouse Scroll Down* to zoom out.

Aligning tracks

When using multiple tracks, there's always some tweaking that you will need to do so that all of the sounds align properly. You might not want to shift the tracks, but instead *align* them to a starting point. There are a number of alignment options in the **Tracks** menu.

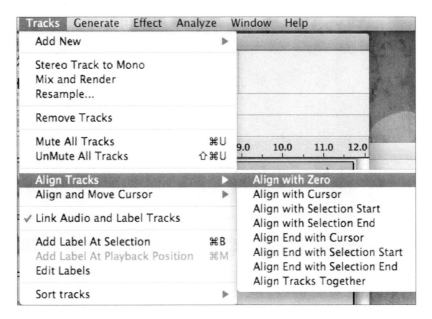

Here's what you can do:

- Align the selected tracks to start when the time is zero
- Align the selected tracks to start or end at the cursor position
- Align the start or end of the selected tracks with the start or end of a selection
- Align all of the tracks together

One thing to note is that the last option in the previous list only synchronizes the audio of the tracks if the audio starts at the start of the tracks.

We'll do one example here, to help get you started. To align the tracks to start at the cursor position you would:

1. Select the tracks that you want to align in your Audacity project by clicking and dragging your cursor over the timelines. You'll notice that an arrow appears at the top of your timeline, showing where the cursor start is.

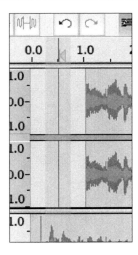

2. On the main menu, select **Tracks** and then **Align Tracks | Align with Cursor**.

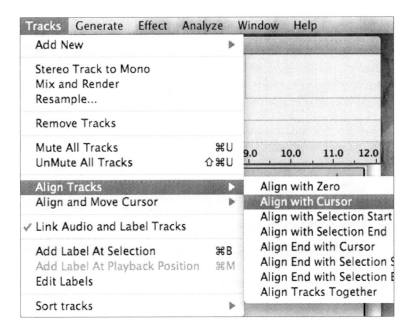

The first selected audio track moves to your cursor position. The other audio tracks in the project are also moved an equal distance as the selected track was moved, so that all tracks stay aligned.

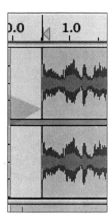

Splitting and duplicating audio

When you **split** an audio track, it removes the selected area from the original, creates another track, and places the selected area into it—in essence creating another audio track. This is useful when you want to re-order the audio in a different sequence than the one in which it was originally recorded.

Using **duplicate** is similar, but instead of removing the selection from the original track, it just duplicates the selected audio into a new track. Both of these features create new audio tracks—it just depends if the selected area in the original was removed from it (splitting) or just copied to another track (duplicating).

Splitting tracks

Splitting audio tracks is most often used to make multiple audio clips—or short pieces of audio—that are going to be re-ordered or moved around from their original recorded order. You can split tracks in a few different ways.

Split and Time Shift

The first technique allows you to literally "split" the sound waves, and make a breaking point at different points in the timeline . You can then use the **Time Shift** tool to manually move sections to another point in the same track, or even to another track. Here's how it's done:

1. In an Audacity project, place your cursor at a point in the timeline where you want to split the track.

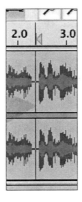

2. From the main menu, select **Edit**, and then **Split**.

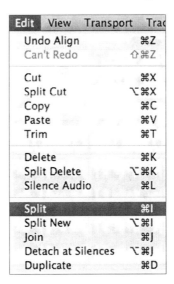

You'll see a break (or split) in the audio, which is now shown as two separate audio clips.

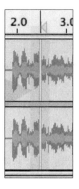

 You can also use the **Selection Tool** and select a portion of the audio track, and then select **Edit** and then **Split**. This creates two breaks — one at the beginning of the selection and one at the end.

3. Select the **Time Shift Tool**, and manually move each split in the timeline, or even into another audio track altogether.

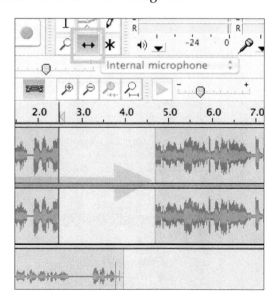

Note that, each time you make a split, you will leave a break in your timeline.

Split and cut

This form of splitting takes a selected portion of the audio track, removes it from the original timeline, and lets you paste it somewhere else in the timeline (or into another audio track). Here's how it's done:

1. From an open project, select a section of audio in the timeline.

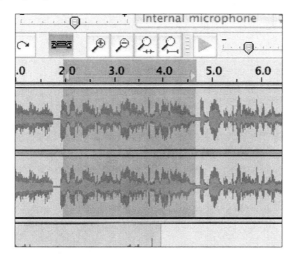

2. On the main menu select **Edit** and then **Split Cut**.

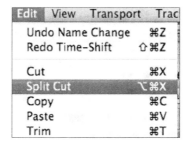

The selected audio is cut from the track, leaving silence.

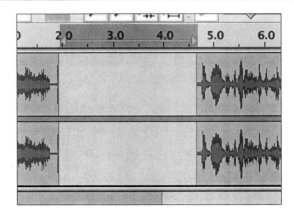

4. Place the cursor at any point in the current timeline, or in a new track, and then select **Edit** and then **Paste**. The cut audio is pasted into the selected audio track. For this example, we pasted into another track. You will notice in the screen capture that the clip is pasted into a new track at the same point in the timeline.

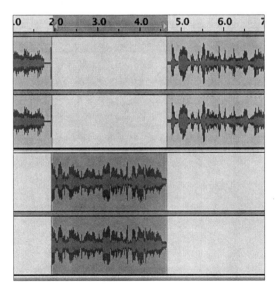

Split Delete

Using the **Split Delete** menu item removes the selected section of audio from the track, and creates silence for the selected area. The selected area then is literally deleted from the audio track entirely (unlike split cut, where you can then paste the removed audio clip into another track). Here's how this works:

1. Select a piece of audio in the timeline.

2. From the main menu, select **Edit** and then **Split Delete**.

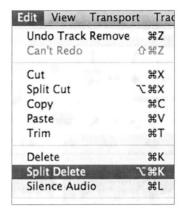

You'll see that the selected portion of the audio is deleted and replaced with silence in the timeline.

 If you select only a portion of the audio track, and use the **Delete** key on your keyboard, Audacity acts differently. It actually takes the remaining audio pieces and joins them together back into one continuous audio track.

Duplicating tracks

If you want to experiment with effects or sounds, sometimes it might be best to **duplicate** a track or a portion of the audio track. When you do this, the selected area essentially gets copied, and a new track is automatically created with the duplicated area pasted into it in the exact same place in the timeline. It's as easy to perform a duplicate as it is for split functions, as shown below.

1. Select a portion of the audio track.

2. From the main menu, select **Edit** and then **Duplicate**.

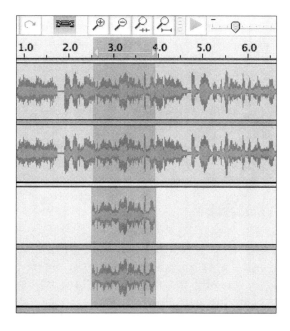

Immediately, you will see that what you have selected is copied or duplicated into a new audio track.

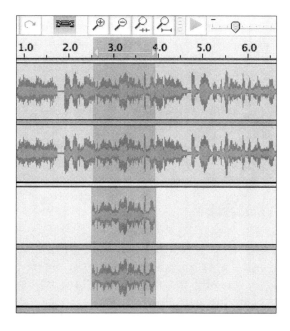

Joining audio tracks

Joining is as simple as it sounds. This function takes two audio clips and joins them together. Typically you would do this if you had split two pieces of audio through editing, or had reordered your audio, and were ready to join them back together into one continuous piece.

A simple join of two clips that are placed next to each other in the timeline is easy to do:

1. In an open project, select the area around a split.

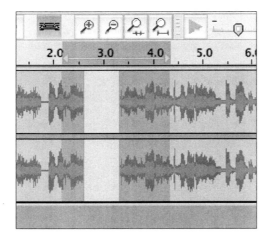

2. Next, from the main menu, select **Edit** and then **Join**.

The split is essentially deleted, and the two separate clips become one.

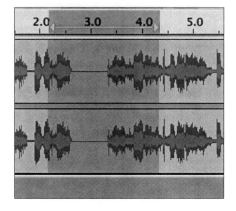

You'll see in the previous screenshot that these two clips are joined but there is silence between them. This is because there was also a time shift between the two clips.

If you wanted the two clips to be joined into a bit more of a seamless join, use the **Time Shift Tool** to move the two clips as close together as possible.

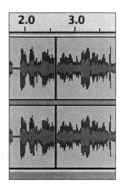

Select **Edit** and **Join**. Now, the two clips are joined into one track again with no silence between them.

Modifying settings for the entire track

Some settings that optimize your audio for the best sound quality require that you perform some track-wide settings. We'll cover a variety here that can be done with your project.

Customize the project rate for each track

In Chapter 1, *Audacity and the World of Audio Editing*, we set the overall project bitrate (the number of computer bits that are conveyed or processed per unit of time). But now, after recording the track, you might want to change the playback rate to create a smaller file size for easier download, or maybe because you don't really need as high a quality as you initially determined.

Changing this setting is easy. In the audio track that you want to change, you just click on the **Track Name** drop down box, select **Set Rate**, and then select the new bitrate you want the audio to be set to.

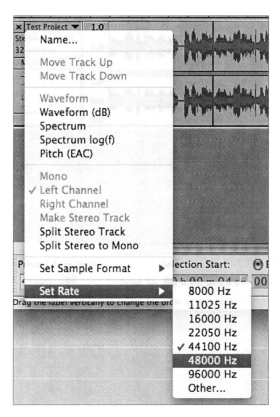

Changing a Stereo track to Mono

For our sample project, we recorded the audio in stereo. You can change the playback to mono to decrease the file size. However, if the start or end positions of a channel are different, or you have split the left or right channels of an audio track already when editing, you won't be able to change over to mono, as the channels have already been edited or split, and so can't be properly converted. To make this change, select the track, and from the main menu select **Tracks** and then **Stereo Track to Mono**.

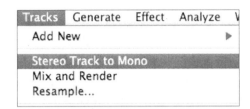

You'll see the audio track change in the project window. What once was two channels of audio, is now one, or a mono channel.

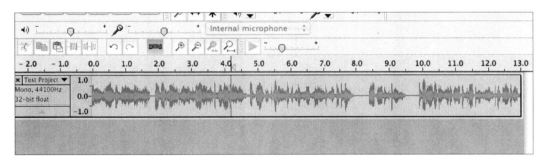

Muting a track

When you work with projects with many audio tracks, you might want to mute a track while editing others, so that it is easy to distinguish what has changed. This is quite easy to do. In the track that you want to mute, just click on the **Mute** button.

The entire track will turn gray, to show that it is muted.

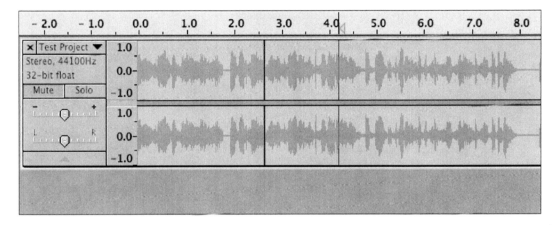

To unmute, you just click on the **Mute** button again, and the track returns to being an active audio track in the project.

Increasing the volume of the entire track

Usually, when you record audio, particularly voice tracks, the volume of the track is low. When you have finished editing and adding effects, you can then **normalize the track**. Normalizing means increasing the overall signal so that the loudest parts of the track are at the peak levels. It's useful to normalize all of your tracks before mixing. This is a very easy process.

1. Select the track that you want to normalize.

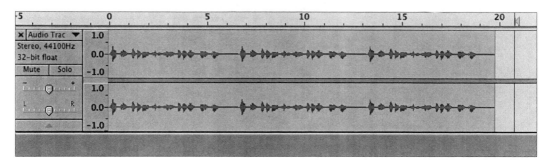

2. Next, from the main menu, select **Effects** and then **Normalize**.

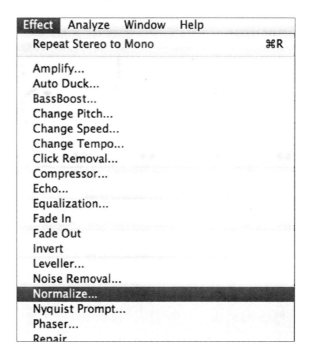

3. Typically, you can just use the defaults on the **Normalize** window and click on **OK**. But here's what each available option means:

   ° Keeping the **Remove any DC offset (center on 0.0 vertically)** checked makes sure that any vertical displacement of the track is "centered"

   ° Using the **Normalize maximum amplitude to** setting lets you set the maximum amplitude decibel level to a fixed amount

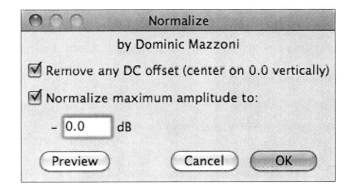

4. You'll see that the voice waves on the timeline are now bigger, thus increasing the volume.

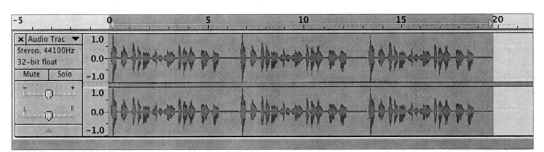

 The human ear can only sense about a 6 dB increase or decrease in any two volume samples. That being said, play a bit with these settings to explore what works for your track, and what can actually be heard, with headphones or speakers, when normalizing.

Sorting tracks

In Audacity, it's possible to have projects with multiple tracks. The more tracks you have, the more you might have a need to sort them in a way that makes sense for your editing. For example, if you sort your tracks by start time all tracks will be put into the same sequence in which they will be played back once your project is exported. It can give you a clear way to listen, and determine if your editing is working.

You can also sort by name. This is useful if you have many tracks with similar names—such as `InterviewPart1`, `InterviewPart2`, `InterviewPart3`. You can then easily adjust the order in which your audio tracks will be heard.

To sort tracks, all you need to do is:

1.   Open an Audacity project.

2.   On the main menu, select **Tracks** and then **Sort Tracks**.

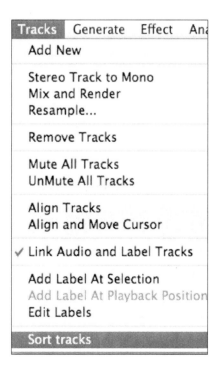

3.   From this menu, you can choose to sort **by Name** or **by Start time**.

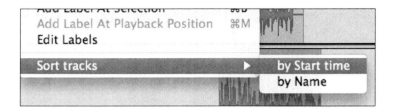

Your tracks will be sorted as specified, and you can continue editing, or testing how the playback will sound.

Summary

We have covered a lot of advanced editing features in this chapter. We learned to soften sibilants, how to clip and replace sounds, how to perform time shifts, and how to align audio tracks. We also learned how to split and join tracks, how to normalize (or increase the entire track volume), how to mute tracks, and even how to sort them for easy playback and editing. All of these are advanced editing techniques that you might want to try in your future Audacity projects. In the next chapter, we'll look at adding background music, overdubbing, and fading in and out, in order to give your project even more depth.

8

Importing and Adding Background Music

You can use Audacity to import music into your project, convert different audio files from one format to another, bring in multiple files and convert them, and more. In this chapter, we will learn how to add background music into your podcast, overdub, and fade in and out. We will also discuss some additional information about importing music from CDs, cassette tapes, and vinyl records.

Importing digital music into Audacity

Before you can add background music to any Audacity project, you'll first have to import a digital music file into to the project itself.

Importing WAV, AIFF, MP3, and MP4/M4A files

Audacity can import a number of music file formats. WAV, AIFF, MP3 are most common, but it can also import MP4/M4A files, as long as they are not rights-managed or copy-protected (like some songs purchased through stores such as iTunes). To import a song into Audacity:

1. Open your sample project.

2. From the main menu, select **File**, **Import**, and then **Audio**.

The audio selection window is displayed.

3. Choose the music file from your computer, and then click on **Open**. A new track is added to your project at the very bottom of the project window.

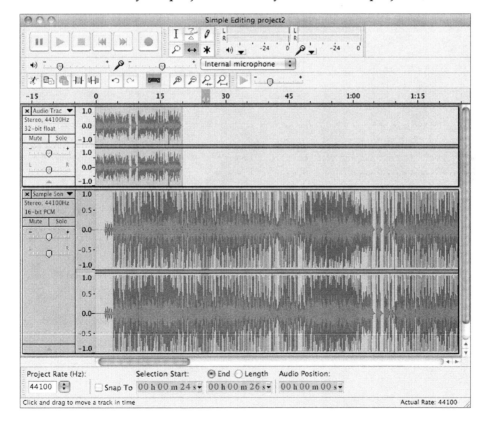

Importing music from iTunes

Your iTunes library can contain protected and unprotected music files. The main difference is that the protected files were typically purchased from the iTunes store and can't be played outside of that software. There is no easy way to determine visually which music tracks are protected or unprotected, so you can try both methods outlined next to import into Audacity. However, remember there are copyright laws for songs written and recorded by popular artists, so you need to investigate how to use music legally for your own use or for distribution through a podcast.

Unprotected files from iTunes

If the songs that you want to import from iTunes aren't copy-protected, importing them is easy. Click-and-drag the song from the iTunes window and drop it into your Audacity project window (with your project open, of course).

Within a few moments, the music track is shown at the bottom of your project window.

The music track is now ready to be edited in, as an introduction or however you desire, in the main podcast file. If this is that all you need to do, feel free to skip to the *Adding Background Music to your Project* section later in this chapter.

Protected files from iTunes

If you are producing a podcast for your own use only, and want to import purchased music from iTunes, moving it into Audacity is a bit more complicated, since these files are typically in a protected file format (that is, they are not playable outside of the iTunes software). Before you can use them in Audacity, you will need to extract them in an unprotected format. We'll discuss how you can burn an audio CD and do this.

 You can also use royalty free music downloaded from web sites like Jamendo (http://www.jamendo.com/). This music is free and can be legally used and distributed in podcasts. See the website for more details.

Burn a CD and extract from it

You'll need to do a few things to be able to create an audio CD in iTunes for this to work: Create a playlist including the song (or songs) that you want to add to your podcast, then burn it to an audio CD (AIFF format) using the iTunes software itself. Generally, using these steps does not result in a loss of sound quality. Here's all the detailed steps:

1. To keep the highest quality of the songs we need to change a setting in iTunes. Open iTunes, and in the Windows operating system go to the **Edit** menu and select **Preferences,** or on a Mac go to the **iTunes** menu and choose **Preferences.**

2. In the **General** tab, select **Importing Settings.**

3. In the **Import** window, choose AIFF Encoder and then click on **OK.** Even though these settings say they are for importing CD content, the same settings apply for creating CDs.

4. Now it is time to find the song (or songs) that you want to incorporate into your Audacity project, and place a blank burnable CD into the CD drive of your computer.

5. Then, from the iTunes main menu, select **File** and **New Playlist.**

6. Enter a playlist name, and then press *Enter*.

7. Drag the song (or songs) that you want to import into Audacity into this playlist.

8. Select the playlist, and then click on the **Burn Disc** button on the lower-right of the iTunes window.

The **Burn Settings** window is displayed.

9. Select **Audio CD**, and then click on **Burn**. You'll see the CD burning progress in the iTunes progress bar.

10. When it is complete, you can display the contents of the CD itself and see all the music files in M4A form.

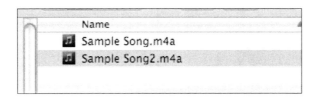

11. You can now drag the song file to the open Audacity project window. The music track will appear at the bottom of this screen.

Now the music track is ready to be edited in, as an introduction or however you desire, in the main podcast file. Feel free to skip to the *Adding background music* section later in this chapter to get started!

Adding music to your podcast

Adding music to your podcast can give it more depth—even if you just add it in the introduction and when you are ending the podcast. But, as discussed earlier in the chapter, there are copyright laws for songs written and recorded by popular artists, so you need to investigate how to use music properly in your podcasts for distribution.

You've already imported your music in the previous steps. If you remember, Audacity imports the music file into your project and puts it in its own stereo track. Now let's piece them all together through some editing.

Timing the music for introductions and endings

Right now, with the new music track added into your project window, if you click on **Play**, you will see that Audacity mixes the music and voice track for you—playing both tracks at the same time (or all tracks, if you have more than two). To start, we're going to explain how to create a music introduction and ending.

For this example, we'll have the music start *before* we hear the podcast content and then have it continue a bit *after* the voice track ends as seen in the next screenshot. However, you can set up your podcast to be structured however you like. Some podcasts start with a brief, vocal only description of the podcast, and then move into a musical introduction.

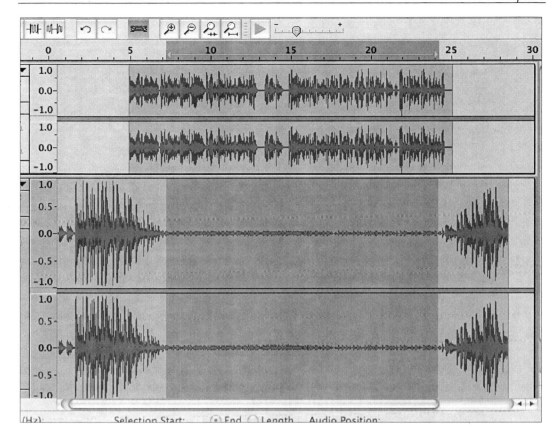

If you remember, in the previous chapter we discussed the **Time Shift Tool**. We'll be using it again here to move the start time of our voice track to later in the timeline. That way, we'll hear some of the music first.

1. In the open Audacity project with your music track imported, select the voice track (your podcast with recorded voice) and then select the **Time Shift Tool**.

2. Move the track to start about 10 to 15 seconds into the timeline. Use the zoom tool if you need to see the timeline clearer.

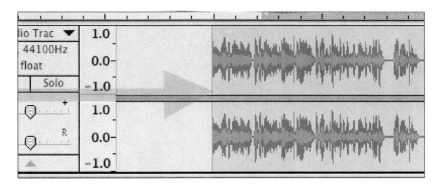

3. Click on **Skip to Start** and then click on the **Play** button, to hear how this intro sounds. Does the narration start at a good break in the music?

You'll notice that right now the music still plays in the background of the voice track. It is probably too loud to stay that way. For now, we're going to learn to do some additional fading in and out of the music and silence the rest.

Fading in and out

Next, we'll fade out the music behind the narration for the introduction and then fade the music back in for a closing of the podcast.

1. From where we left off in the last set of steps, let's fade out the music so we'll be able to hear the voice track. Select the music track in the Audacity project window.

2. Click on the **Select Tool**, and select a small portion of the music track that starts just before the voice track begins, and that ends a little into the audio.

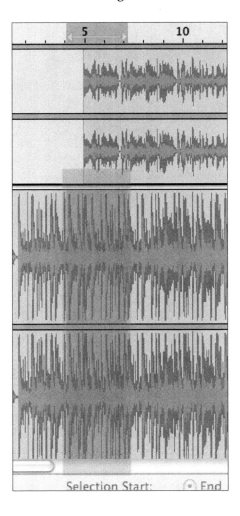

3. Next, from the Audacity main menu, select **Effect** and then **Fade Out**.

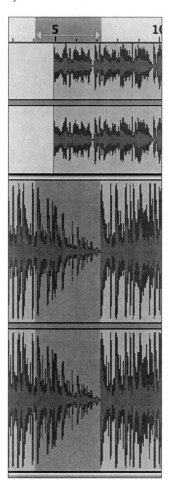

You'll notice that the sound waves in that selected portion will go from large to small (loud to soft), and eventually to silence.

4. Next, we're going to select a portion of the music track near the end of the voice track. Select from a short while before the voice track ends to a short while after.

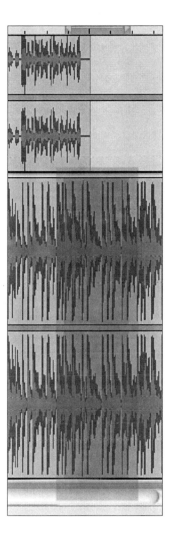

5. Select **Effect** and then **Fade In** from the main menu. This time, you will see that the sound waves in the selected area will change to show a small to large (soft to loud) transition.

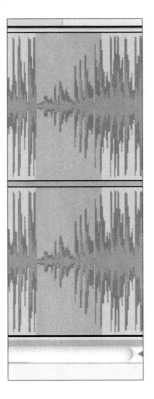

6. Next, we're going to silence the middle portion of the music so that we can hear this entire project in full. Select the portion of the music track that is between the Fade Out and In sections.

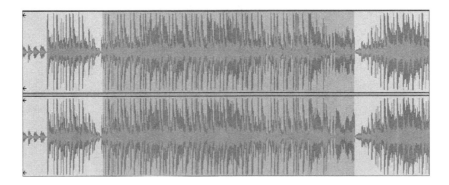

7. Click on the **Silence** button.

You will see the sound waves change to a straight line, which means that this portion is silent.

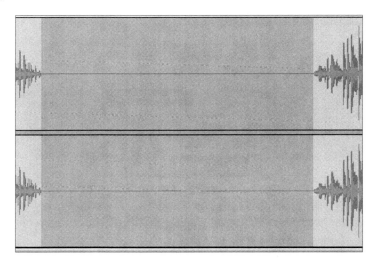

8. Go back to the start of the entire track by clicking on the **Skip to Start** button and click on the **Play** button. You should hear the music introduction that nicely fades to the vocal part of the podcast, and then transitions again at the end by fading in some music and then ending.

9. Refer to the next section if you want to have background music play while speaking throughout your podcast, or select **File** and **Save** to save the project this way.

Adding background music

In the previous example, we simply silenced the music so that all that was heard was the vocal track. But what if you want to have music playing softly in the background *during* the voice portion? There is a very simple way to do this.

1. Follow steps 1 to 5 from *Fading in and out* to get the music positioned at the correct timeline location and the fading in and out done correctly, but don't silence the music during the voice track. Instead, go to the main menu and select **Effect** and then **Amplify**.

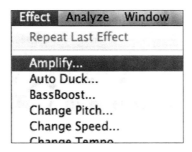

The **Amplify** window is displayed. Essentially, we are going to decrease (lower) the volume of the music during this portion of the podcast.

2. Move the slider to the left to lower the volume. You might try moving it in a range of -10 to -12 dB to start with.

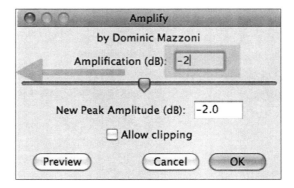

You do not want to increase amplification (move the slider to the right) here. If you try, you are actually increasing the volume, and the background music will bury the voice track. In fact, if you try to do this, the **OK** button will become disabled. Always move the slider to the left.

4. Click on **OK**. You'll notice that the overall height of the sound waves in that area becomes smaller.

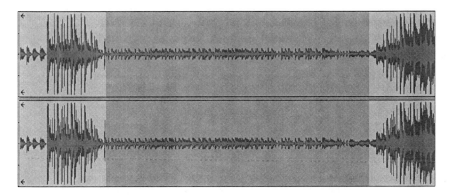

5. Now move to the start of your timeline and click on the **Play** button. Does the volume level behind the voice track sound OK?

6. If it is still too loud you can undo (from the main menu select **Edit** and **Undo Amplify**) the last change and repeat these steps until it sounds right.

7. Again, if you are happy with the results here, remember to select **File** and then **Save**, in order to keep your work!

What is overdubbing and how do I do it?

Overdubbing is much like what you have done previously with the background music, but you can do this with any additional voice tracks or sounds that you want to add to your podcast. Simply, overdubbing is the idea of recording another audio track and placing it "over" the already-existing track. In Audacity, you can even record another audio track starting anywhere within the timeline. To start an overdubbing session:

1. Select where you want the overdub to start, in the current timeline.

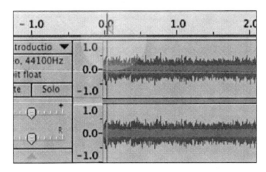

2. Click on the **Record** button to start the overdub. Notice that visually you will see the overdub recording start where you specified, and you will simultaneously hear the audio of the initial audio track as you record the new overdub track. You can talk as you normally would, if you want to add in some additional "side-talk", or you can make some additional sounds (like clapping or walking) to accentuate your "story" in the podcast content track.

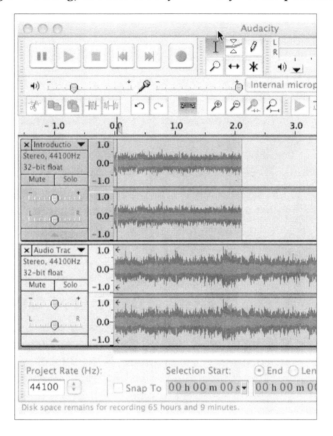

If you don't see a new recording overdub session start where you specified, it is possible you have overdubbing turned off. To turn it on, go to the main menu and look at Transport | Overdub. If there is a check mark by the Overdub option, it is turned on.

3. Click on the **Stop** button when you have finished with the additional sound recording.

4. Again, if you want to play back the entire timeline sequence, select the beginning of the timeline and then click on the **Play** button

5. If you like what you've got, select **File** and then **Save**.

There is obviously a lot more that we can do here to finesse this sound—we can time the music more succinctly so that it matches the tone of the podcast, crossfade between music and the podcast content, use the **Time Shift Tool** and adjust the music and clips of the voice track to work together throughout the entire track. But the essential editing techniques above are a great start!

Downmixing and rendering

All of the steps that we've done previously are the start to performing a mix. Now we can downmix. **Downmixing** is the process of combining many tracks of different types of audio and making it into a single recording. Like the previous examples, we are mixing speech with background music, other audio, and sound effects. You could even add instruments.

Just remember that when you export as one audio file format—in this case, it has been mixed—you won't be able to "break" apart the pieces anymore. This is why we recommend that you keep your Audacity project files!

We explained the export process in Chapter 6, *Saving Projects and Exporting Podcasts*, but the process is given in short here, so that you can make a mix of your new podcast, with all its additional features.

1. With your project window open, from the main menu, select **File** and then **Export.**

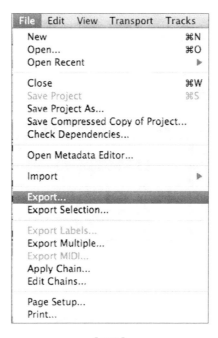

The **Edit Metadata** window is displayed.

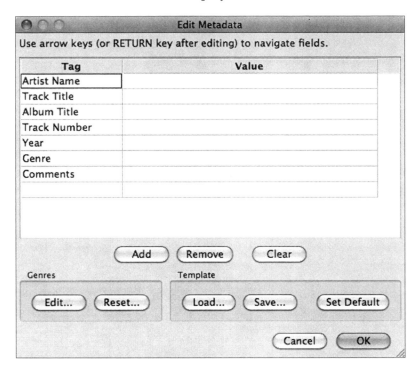

2. Enter tagging information by clicking in the **Value** field of any of the **Tag** fields and enter the required information.

    For example:

    ◦   In **Artist Name**, you could enter your name.

    ◦   In **Track Title**, enter a title for this track (such as Test Podcast).

    ◦   For **Genre**, when you click on the **Value** field, you are offered a drop-down box to choose from a standard list of musical genre options. You can also type in your own special **Genre**.

    ◦   The **Comments** field is free-text, meaning that, you can enter any other relevant information that you would like. An example might be: Interview with Audacity Author detailing how to make a Podcast.

○ You can also add new tags. To do this, click on the **Add** button on this screen. An additional row is added to the table. This has empty **Tag** and **Value** fields for you to use however you would like.

3. Once you have entered all required tags, on the **Edit Metadata** window, click on **OK**. The **Save As** window is displayed.

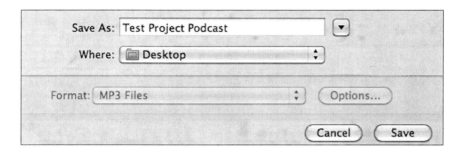

4. Type in a name for the exported file. By default, the project name is entered into the **Save As** field, but you can name the file whatever you like.

5. In the **Where** field, you can choose where you would like the file to be saved.

6. Lastly, in the **Format** field, choose MP3. For your future projects, you can choose any of the available audio formats in this field.

7. Click on **Save**. Your very first MP3 podcast is created and saved!

Want to test it out? Just double-click on the MP3 file that you just saved, and you'll be listening to your new, mixed podcast!

Vinyl records, cassette tapes, or minidiscs

You can use Audacity to record songs from other media, such as vinyl records, cassette tapes, and minidiscs. However this requires a bit of technical knowledge and some trial and error if you've never done it before. You will also need some special equipment, such as:

• A tape deck, minidisc player, or stereo system that has a "line out" connector on the back of it.

- A stereo cable that can connect to the above equipment and then to the "line in" connector on your computer. If you don't have one that fits properly, you can purchase one at almost any electronic store. Just take note of the connector type that you need by looking at your stereo equipment documentation (some types include: mini plugs, RCA, 3.5 mm plug, and so on). Alternatively, you can take the equipment with you to the store and ask for help! Avoid using adapters for connector types, as this is likely to add more noise to your recordings.

- For vinyl records, you need a special turntable that uses a USB cable to connect to your computer. Use the directions with the turntable to connect to your computer, as they are a bit different. Most of these turntables actually come with the Audacity software on a CD-ROM.

Essentially, the steps are:

1. Plug one end of the stereo cable into the "line out" (or headphone) of your tape deck, minidisc player, or stereo system.

2. Plug the other end of the stereo cable into your computer's "line in" connector (for the vinyl record turntable you would use the USB port on your computer).

3. Open Audacity, and then choose **Audacity** and **Preferences** (or **Edit | Preferences** in Windows) from the main menu.

4. Select **Devices** in the left panel, and make sure the **Recording Device** is set to "line-in", or an applicable device.

5. In the Audacity project window, click on the **Record** button and start playing the tape, disc, or record.

6. When the songs are complete, click on the **Stop** button in Audacity.

It is highly recommended that you read additional resources before getting started. In particular, you should read any documentation associated with the specific equipment that you are using to play the original audio, as there might be specific tricks to using this with a computer for digital recording.

Summary

We spent a lot of time in this chapter discussing importing—or bringing in additional audio tracks—into Audacity. We focused on music tracks so that we could go through the detailed steps for adding introduction and closing music, adding background music, and bringing in music tracks from other software libraries. We even discussed at a high level how to bring music from one physical format (like cassette tapes) into digital formats in Audacity. Up next, we're going to learn more about all the advanced effects that we can use.

9

Giving Your Audio Some Depth: Applying Effects

Audio effects let you enhance your audio tracks, manipulate sounds into others, and basically let you make your recording much more than just a voice recording. In this chapter, we'll use effects to make your project sound clearer, crisper, and enhanced for rich sound. However, you can do much more. Audacity has over 20 effects that come as standard in the software. Some of these we've used already, such as Amplify, Fade In or Out, and Noise Removal. We'll review effects at a basic level, and explore even more effects—learn how to use them, and learn how they can help to make your recordings sound even better.

The Effect menu

Clearly identifiable, Audacity's main menu has an **Effect** option. The Effect menu has all of the effects found in Audacity when you install it. These include:

- Amplifying
- Auto Duck
- BassBoost
- Change Pitch
- Change Speed
- Change Tempo
- Click Removal
- Compressor
- Echo
- Equalization

- Fade In
- Fade Out
- Invert
- Leveller
- Noise Removal
- Normalizer
- Phaser
- Repair
- Repeat
- Reverse
- Sliding Time Scale/Pitch Shift
- Truncate Silence
- Wahwah

Many of these we've discussed in the context of our podcast project and how to edit your audio tracks. In this chapter, we'll learn what each of these effects is, re-enforce some of what we learned in earlier chapters, and then discuss other important effects for you to learn when you are just starting to use Audacity. If you see any more effects in this menu, then you've already installed some effect plug-ins. We'll discuss these in the next chapter.

Amplify

Amplify is another term to describe the action of increasing the volume of sound. The word itself is a descendant of the word amplitude, as in wave amplitude. Sounds are actually waves when represented visually. Adjusting amplification is actually working with those sound waves to make them larger or smaller. By using this effect, we can increase, or reduce the volume level of a selected piece of audio. In Chapter 4, *Making It Sound Better: Editing Your Podcast*, we described the steps for reducing the volume of a selection of audio. Next, we'll discuss how to use this effect to increase volume levels (or amplify) in a recording.

1. In an open project, find an area where the volumes are quiet, or where you want to amplify the sound. You can listen to the recording a few times to find this, or visually look at your timeline. Any area where the voice waves aren't as "high" as the others will do.

2. On the **Tools** toolbar, click on the **Select Tool**.

3. Select the section of audio that you want to amplify.

4. On the main menu, select **Effect** and then **Amplify**. The **Amplify** window is displayed.

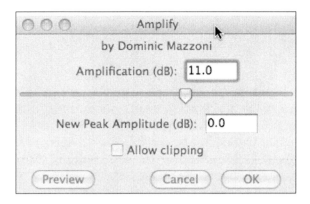

-   ○ If you want to amplify – or turn up the volume of – this selected audio, move the slider to the right, to the higher positive decibel (dB) numbers. The higher the number, the louder the volume.

-   ○ If you want to reduce the volume of this section (decrease the decibel level), then move the slider to the left, to the negative numbers. The greater the negative number, the lower the volume.

-   ○ To test the levels, move the slider to the right about six additional decibels (dB). Your ear can hear about a 6 dB differentiation in volume, so, use steps of 6 dB when adjusting in order to audibly hear the changes that you've made.

5. Click on **Preview**. You'll hear your selected audio at the new decibel or volume level, and can determine if you want to make it even louder (move it to the right even more) or keep this new level.

If you select the **Allow clipping** checkbox, you can amplify the selected audio beyond the highest – or loudest – audio range recorded for this track. So if you want to keep all the audio within the current range, don't select this box, and normalize the audio track.

Using the Normalizer effect increases the amplitude of the recording waveform but does not introduce any new distortion into the recordings. See the details of normalizing a recording later in this chapter.

6. Click on **OK** when you think you've got it right. You can always listen to your project and make sure that it sounds as you expect within the entire audio track. Otherwise, you can "undo" it (on the main menu, select **Edit** and **Undo Amplify**).

Auto Duck

This effect gives you an automatic way to provide background music or sound. It will reduce the volume of one track when there's another playing. Ideally, this can be used to give one track preference over another, in that this track will always sound a bit louder than the other tracks. But be careful, as over-use or improper use of this effect can also have negative affects on the experience of those listening to your podcast. Here's the basics of how to use this effect:

1. Open the Audacity project, with both the music and voice tracks open.

 Make sure that both tracks are timed and aligned correctly, by using the **Time Shift Tool**. You can learn how to do this in Chapter 7, *Beyond the Basics: Editing for Even Better Sound*.

2. Select the track that you want to be quieter than the other. This is, likely the music track.

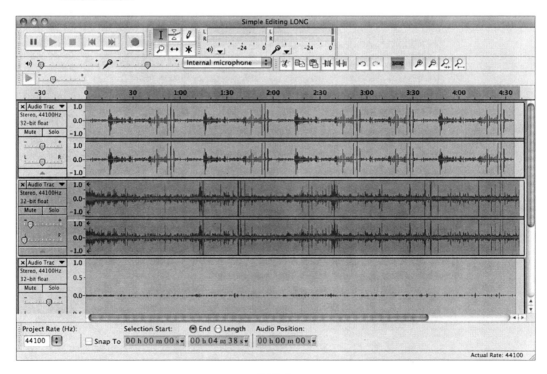

3. On the main menu, select **Effect,** and then **Auto Duck**. The **Auto Duck** window is displayed.

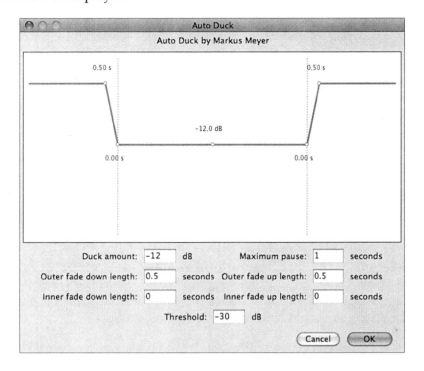

4. Feel free to use the default settings here to test, and simply click on **OK**. Audacity will then analyze the control track (the one that should be louder — the non-selected one)and then apply the effect to the selected track(s). This second portion might take a while to complete because it is actually changing information in that track.

Bass Boost

This effect enhances the bass or lower frequencies in your audio tracks, and is most effective on music tracks. It's very easy to use:

1. With your project open, select the audio track (or a portion of it) that you want to increase the bass sounds.

2. From the main menu, select **Effect** and then **Bass Boost**. The **Bass Boost** window is displayed.

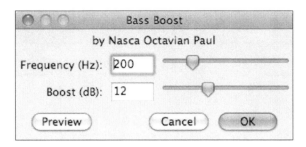

3. Manually specify the amount of bass to be amplified. Typically, 12 dB is a perfect level to start testing.

Pitch

We discussed pitch in Chapter 5, *Fixing the Glitches and Removing the Noise*, but let's define it again. Sounds are regular, even-spaced waves of air molecules. Adjusting the spacing and length of the sounds waves will change the tone or pitch of the sound, making it higher or lower (like male and female voices).

By doing this, we're also decreasing the time between the voice waves (which means we are increasing frequency). Normally, making this change would also increase the speed or tempo of the entire track, but with Audacity, you can change this pitch setting without changing the speed of your audio track. Audacity will re-adjust to maintain the original speed.

To change the pitch:

1. Open up your test project, and select the portion for which you want to change the pitch (or select the entire track).

2. From the main menu, select **Effect** and then **Change Pitch**. The **Change Pitch** window displays.

3. The easiest way to change the pitch of any voice track, is to just use the slider bar along the bottom of the screen. Move this to the left-hand side to lower the pitch, and to the right-hand side to make the pitch higher.

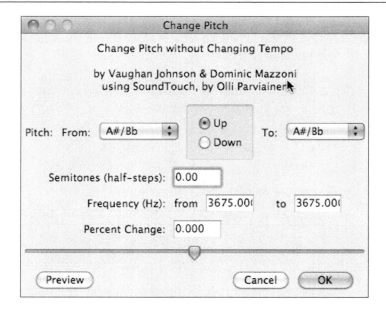

4. To see how you changed the sound, click on the **Preview** button.

5. Click on **OK** when you are satisfied with the setting, and the pitch of the selection will be changed.

Speed

If you want to change the speed of your audio track there is a way to do that, too. However, this will also change the pitch (see *Tempo*, next) *and* shorten your overall track length, because you are literally making the audio track play faster.

To change the speed of your audio track:

1. Open up your test project, and select the portion for which you want to change the speed of playback.

2. From the main menu, select **Effect** and then **Change Speed**. The **Change Speed** window is displayed.

3. Again, the easiest way to change this setting to your liking is to move the slider bar. Move it to the left-hand side to slow down the speed, and to the right-hand side to make it faster.

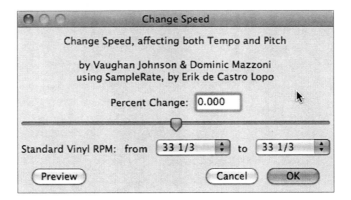

4. Again, you can preview how you changed the sound by clicking on the **Preview** button.

5. Click on **OK** when you are satisfied with the setting, and the pitch of the selection will be changed.

Tempo

You can also increase the speed of one portion of the audio track, but not change the pitch of anything else (like your voice track). To do this, you use the **Change Tempo** effect. Here's the simple steps to do this:

1. Open up your test project, and select the portion for which you want to change the tempo.

2. From the main menu, select **Effect** and then **Change Tempo**. The **Change Tempo** window is displayed.

3. The slider bar is the easiest and fastest way to change this setting. Move it to the left to slow down the tempo, and to the right to make it faster.

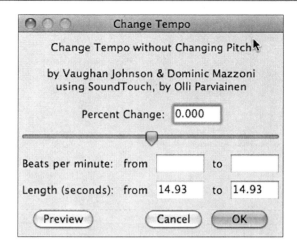

4. Again, you can preview how you changed the sound by clicking on the **Preview** button.

5. Click on **OK** when you are satisfied with the setting, and the pitch of the selection will be changed.

Click Removal

"Clicking" in audio tracks sounds much like what you hear when listening to vinyl records. It is a crack or click sound that can happen when using a faulty microphone, or if you converted your vinyl records to digital sounds using Audacity.

You can use the **Click Removal** effect to remove individual clicks on an audio track. Audacity analyzes the digital form of the audio waves and looks for spikes, removes the spike, and takes a bit of the sound before and after to reconstruct the waveform again. Here's how it works:

1. In an open Audacity project, select part of a track that has the clicking sounds.

2. You can also select an entire track of audio to fix as well, but this effect works better on smaller selections of the audio track. Select only the portion of audio that surrounds the clicking sound.

3. From the main menu, select **Effect** and then **Click Removal**. The **Click Removal** window is displayed.

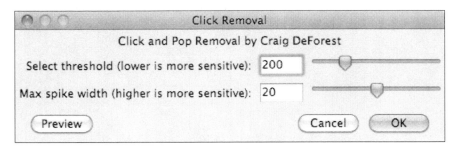

4. For the threshold setting, move the slider to the left or right. Audacity looks at the length of a spike to determine if it is a click. The more to the right, the higher the spike must be to be considered a spike. Farther to the left, the lower the spike requirement.

5. When you are ready, click on the **Remove Clicks** button.

Compressor

In Chapter 5, *Fixing the Glitches and Removing the Noise*, we discussed the compressor effect and how to use it to even out the sound of an audio track. We'll review it again, here. You use this effect if you don't want sudden loud noises or an outburst of a background noise. This effect is similar to the normalizer effect that adjusts the sound levels on the entire track, but compressor only adjusts "strange" noises.

1. In an open project, use the **Selection Tool** to highlight a section of the audio track that needs volume levels evened.

2. Then, from the main menu, select **Effect** and then **Compressor**. The **Dynamic Range Compressor** window is displayed.

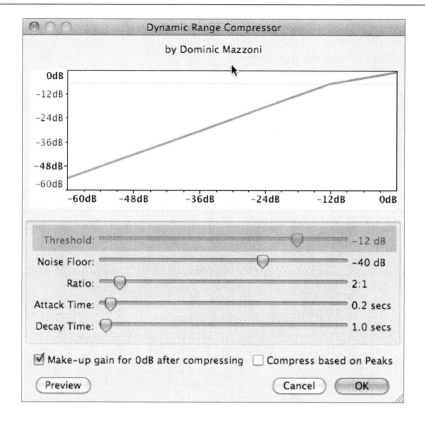

3. We'll focus on setting the **Threshold**—or the maximum volume that we want for the entire audio track. Once this setting is determined, any part of the audio that is louder than the set threshold will have its volume reduced. Set the threshold somewhere between the loudest and softest parts of your audio.

4. The next setting is **Ratio**, which sets the level of compression. Typically, the default setting of 2:1 works well, but you can adjust this setting as necessary to. The higher the first number, the more compression (volume adjusting) that happens.

5. Test your **Attack Time** setting. This tells Audacity how fast to apply your compression ratio. For voice recordings, 0.2 generally works best as a general rule of thumb. However, it can sometimes make the sound un-natural.

6. Again, we will leave **Make-up Gain for 0dB after compressing** selected. This is important, as it increases the overall volume of the recording in its entirety.

7. When you're all set, click on the **Preview** button to hear what your audio track will sound like.

8. If you like the result, click on **OK** for the compression process to complete. This could take a couple seconds or a few minutes, depending on how large of a selection you chose to adjust.

Echo

Just as you would expect, this effect creates an echo in your audio. It does this by taking the selected audio and repeating it, optionally getting lower in volume with each repetition. Ready to try it? It's simple:

1. In an open Audacity project, select the audio that you want to echo.

2. From the main menu, select **Effect** and then **Echo**. The **Echo** window displays.

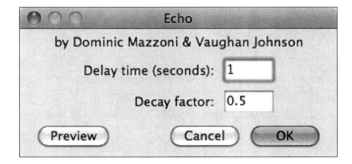

3. Set the delay between echos, in seconds, remembering that you should set this to any number greater than 0 (setting it to 0 wouldn't create any echo at all).

4. Next is the **Decay factor**. This is the setting that determines how much softer the repeat is of the original, in each "round" of the echo. If you set this to 0, there will be no echo because the repeat would be as loud as the original. If you set this to 0.5 the volume is cut in half on each repetition.

5. Once these two settings are set, click on **OK** to create the echo.

Equalization

Just like with your home stereo, you can change the Bass, Treble and Balance information captured in your voice track recording—all considered frequency types in audio. **Equalization** is the process of manipulating these frequencies by increasing some and decreasing others, in order to get the desired sound that you want, and for the best audio from a wide range of speaker options. To access the **Equalization** settings, go to the main menu and select **Effect** and then **Equalization**.

A graph is displayed, showing all of the detailed equalization factors.

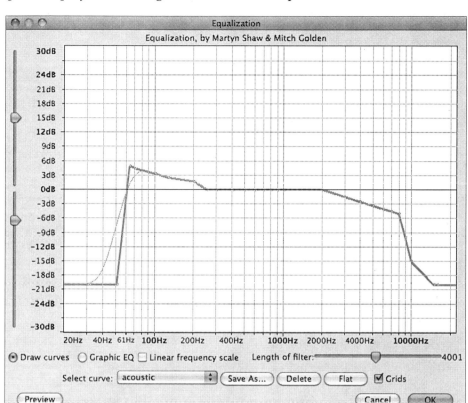

The previous graph is the "Curve" view of Equalization. You can also view this information in a Graphic or Bar view, or a Linear View. Let's discuss the Curve view first.

Because this is a graph it has a vertical axis along the left-most side and a horizontal axis along the bottom. The **Vertical** focuses on the amplification gain in the audio, and is in decibels. The **Horizontal** axis or scale is in Hertz, and shows the frequencies where volume adjustments will be made. Bass (low) frequencies are on the left-hand side, midrange frequencies in the middle, and the treble (high) frequencies are on the right-hand side.

The two lines within the graph are blue and green curves. The blue line has a number of white circles, or **control points** that are moveable. Click-and-drag any control point up to increase the volume of that frequency, or down to decrease the volume (or drag a control point off the graph completely to remove it).

So, if you want to increase the bass, you can move a control point on the left-hand side of the graph upward to make the change. Decreasing treble, or high frequencies would mean taking control points on the right-hand side of the graph and moving them downward.

You'll see the changes happen on the thick blue curve immediately. The thin green curve is actually what Audacity uses to process the equalization effect. It attempts to keep the thin green curve as close to the thick blue curve as possible, but will adjust if there are sudden changes in amplitude or frequencies.

You can also use the **Graphic EQ** (Equalization) mode to make adjustments to the thick blue line a bit more easily. You just move sliders up and down—much like a home stereo equalizer—and switch back to the Curve mode, and you will see that the thick blue line has changed to reflect the changes you made.

Here's some general guidelines to look at to get started with equalization:

- For more rich and full sound, increase or amplify bass frequencies.
- Increase the volume of treble frequencies to create a more clear sound.
- Change frequencies in small steps until you like the sound of what you hear.
- Try adding treble for each frequency. If you don't hear improvements, then switch to bass and try the same.
- Adjusting frequencies for voice will require some testing. If frequencies are set too low, the voices will sound "boomy", too high, they can sound too hollow. Try to decrease the low frequencies and increasing in the 1 to 5 kilohertz range for a bit more clarity.

Using Equalization is really a matter of trail and error. It takes a practiced ear and practical experience for finding out what best works for your recording environment. Listen carefully, test and manipulate to find the best sound.

Fading In and Out

As we explained in Chapter 8, *Importing and Adding Background Music*, you can use Fade In and Out for background music. Here's the basics about how you'd use either feature (but feel free to refer to Chapter 8, *Importing and Adding Background Music*, for all the little details).

1. From an audio track, use the **Select Tool**, and select a small portion of the audio track.

2. Next, from the Audacity main menu, select **Effect** and then **Fade Out** or **Fade In**. The sound waves in the selected portion will go from large to small (loud to soft) and eventually to silence, or vice versa, if you chose to Fade In.

Invert

For basic podcasting you may never use this effect, but it is fun nonetheless. Invert flips the selected audio upside-down. Feel free to try it and experiment.

1. From an audio track, use the **Select Tool**, and select a small portion of the audio track.

2. Next, from the Audacity main menu, select **Effect** and then **Invert**. You'll see the selected audio flip upside down. In many instances you might find this doesn't even change your audio sounds at all.

Leveller

Leveller works a bit different than the Compressor effect—but does something similar to the sound. As the name suggests, it takes quiet parts of the audio track and makes them louder and the louder parts quieter. But it can introduce some distortion. It's possible that when you recorded your interview in Audacity that the recording is much louder when you, the interviewee is speaking, and much softer when your interviewer on the phone is responding. Using the leveller effect would take those sounds and adjust them so they sound more equal in their volume.

Here's how to give the leveller effect a try:

1. From an audio track, use the **Select Tool**, and select a small portion of the audio track.

2. Next, from the main menu, select **Effect** and then **Leveller**.

Noise removal

Noise can be hisses and hums heard in the background of your audio track. As discussed in Chapter 5, *Fixing the Glitches and Removing the Noise*, this effect will analyze your audio track, after you tell it what is considered "noise", and will compare it to all of the other sounds. If the noise profile is "heard" it silences it in the track and lets the other noise types remain. Here's the details of how to do this entire process:

Setting up the noise profile

We need to tell Audacity what is considered noise. So, we'll be selecting a portion of the audio that is silent except for the noise.

1. Open your Audacity sample project. Find a section of the audio file where there is noise and only noise.

2. Use the **Selection Tool** to select that portion of silence to teach Audacity what is considered quiet.

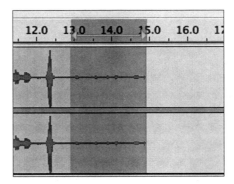

3. On the main menu, select **Effect** and **Noise Removal**. The **Noise Removal** screen is displayed.

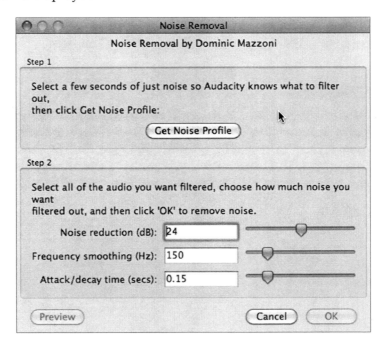

4. Click on the **Get Noise Profile** button.

5. Depending on the size of the sample that you selected, this can take anywhere from one second to a few seconds. When the window disappears you are ready to move to the next part of the process.

You've just set your noise profile and are now ready for part two of noise removal.

Removing the noise

We are now ready to actually analyze the entire audio track and get rid of the noise.

1. In the same project where you just set the noise profile, select the entire audio track—for the entire timeline. You can select by clicking and dragging across the entire timeline, or by pressing *Command + A* (or in Windows *Ctrl + A*) on your keyboard.

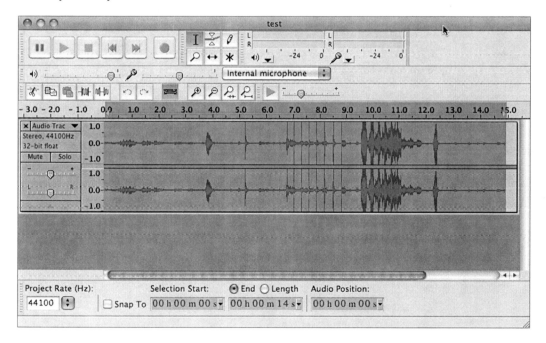

2. On the main menu, select **Effect** and then **Noise Removal** again.

3. You'll see the **Noise Removal** screen again. This time, look at the top slider, **Noise reduction**.

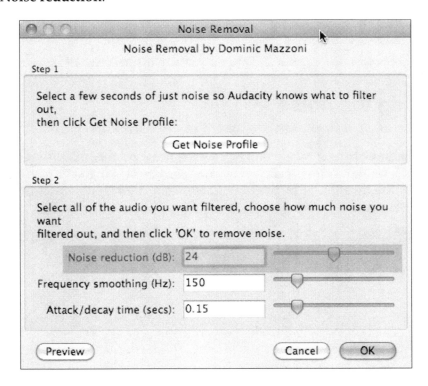

You can move this slider to the left-hand side (for less) or to the right-hand side (for more), depending on how much noise you want to remove.

4. Ready to hear a preview? Then click on the **Preview** button to hear how the current settings would change the audio. If it isn't to your liking, then re-adjust the slider, and click on **Preview** again.

Hearing an Echo?

Moving the **Noise Reduction** slider too far to the right-hand side can give you an echo in place of the noise. Moving the slider just left of center works best.

5. When you like what you hear in the preview, click on **OK**. Once again, depending on the length of your entire audio track, this could take from a few seconds to many minutes.

6. Again, because the preview is a very short test, play the entire file to make sure that it sounds the way that you like. Click on the **Play** button, and listen.

7. If, for any reason, you don't like what you hear, undo the noise removal by selecting **Edit** from the main menu, and then select **Undo Noise Removal**.

Normalizer

This is a great setting if you just want to make all of your audio tracks as loud as possible. Basically, you are forcing them all to be the same volume, and as loud as they can be. It's easy to set it up this way.

1. Open your project.
2. Go to the main menu, and select **Effect** and then **Normalize**.
3. Use the defaults on this screen, and click on **OK**.

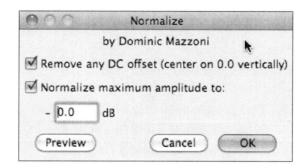

This is a safe effect, in that it will never make your sample so loud as to introduce distortion. It's one of the easiest ways to increase your volume!

Phaser

At a basic level, the phaser effect gives the audio track an oscillating sound. The settings for this function can be a bit tricky, but this is also a great effect to use for podcast introductions and fade-ins. Use and test all of the settings. It offers a unique effect and will teach you about the parameters used in many of the effects in Audacity. Here's how it's done:

1. From an open Audacity project, select the track (or portion of it) to which you would like to add this effect.

2. On the main menu, choose **Effect** and then **Phaser**. The **Phaser** window is displayed.

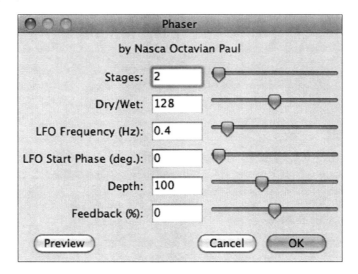

3. From this window, there are six settings that you can manipulate. Here's what each of these settings is along with some directions on how to set them:

    ○ **Stages**—The higher the number here, the more rapid the oscillating sound

    ○ **DRY/WET**—Specifies how much of the original (dry) sound is heard versus the amount that has the effect (wet)

    ○ **LFO (Low-Frequency Oscillator) Frequency**—Number of times to process the signal in a second

    ○ **LFO Start Phase**—The starting place for the oscillation

    ○ **Depth**—The higher this number the deeper the oscillation sound.

    ○ **Feedback**—The percentage or amount that the oscillation should rotate through (as in how much feedback, as the name suggests)

4. Click on **OK** when you want to set this effect. Play back the audio track to hear how it sounds!

Repair

When you use the repair effect in Audacity, it is really only for an area that needs to be fixed. Maybe it wasn't recorded properly, or there was an error in how your equipment picked up the audio. In any case, you select only the "broken" portion of the track to repair. Here's the details:

1. Select the "broken" part of the audio track, or the glitch.

2. From the main menu, select **Effect** and then **Repair**.

3. Audacity analyzes the audio wave from before and after the damaged portion and then "fixes" it—or, more technically, extrapolates the wave to make it continuous—so that it is repaired.

Other ways to help hide a repair is to decrease the volume for the repaired area (by using the Amplify effect), or duck it with another track (the Auto Duck effect). Both of these options will make the problem area less noticeable during playback.

Repeat

As the name suggests, this effect will repeat the audio track (or selected section of audio) the specified number of times. Here's how it is done.

1. With an open project, select the audio track (or a portion of it) that you want to repeat.

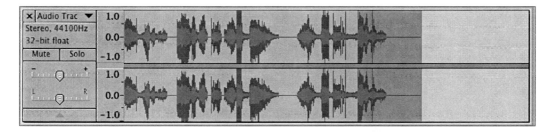

2. From the main menu, select **Effect** and then **Repeat**. The **Repeat** window is displayed.

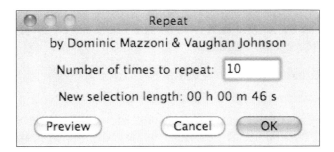

3. Set the *number of times* that you want the sound to be repeated. If, for any reason, you need it set to repeat to a specific amount of time (say for 2 minutes), you'll need to take the initial audio track length and figure out how many times it would need to be repeated to make 2 minutes. For example, if your track is 10 seconds long, you would need to repeat it 12 times to equal 2 minutes of time.

4. Click on **OK** when complete, and you will see that your audio track repeats itself and will now be the new length.

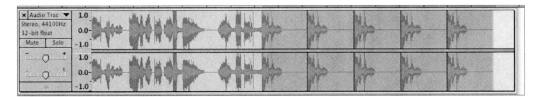

This effect is often confused with Echo. It differs from echo because:

- There is a delay between repetitions. In this example, there would be a longer silence between segments instead of a true copy of the original.

- You would see a visual decrease in amplitude (which will make the wave length heights decrease with each echo repeat).

Reverse

Reverse is an interesting effect. It literally reverses the sound, so that you hear it backwards—the end of the audio will be heard first, and the beginning last. Why would this be done? Sometimes it is a way to "hide" or "bleep" out crude language, or can represent "rewinding" or "going back in time". It's an easy effect to try:

1. With an open project, select the audio track that you want to reverse.

2. From the main menu, select **Effect** and then **Reverse**. Within a few minutes, your track will have been reversed. Now you can export this as it's own MP3 file.

Sliding Time Scale/Pitch Shift

Usually, when you change the pitch of an audio track, it will change the tempo, and vice versa. However, this effect actually allows you to simultaneously change the pitch without changing the tempo, and the tempo without changing the pitch. Or you can change both at varying rates. Let's see how this is done:

1. Open a project, and select an audio track.

2. From the main menu, select **Effect** and then **Sliding Time Scale/Pitch Shift**. The **Time Scale** window is displayed.

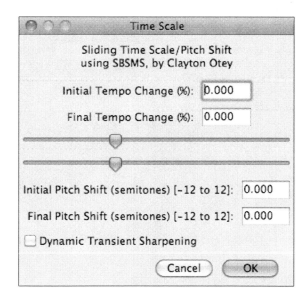

3. You'll see both tempo change settings and pitch shift settings. Adjust the settings to experiment with the sound.

4. If you select the **Dynamic Transient Sharpening** check box, you are turning this feature on. This means that you are giving Audacity the ability to adjust the tempo, based on the frequency of the audio content. When the frequency of the audio content increases rapidly, it stretches the content less, and then compensates by stretching the audio content more when the frequency of the audio content is not changing.

6. Click on **OK** when your changes are complete, to hear the full audio track with the new settings.

Truncate Silence

This effect will automatically delete silences of a specified length. This can be helpful if you are recording a podcast and take long breaks between sections in the podcast. You can then edit the recording in post-production and take the long silences out.

1. Select the audio track that you want to edit.

2. From the main menu, select **Effect** and then **Truncate Silence**. The **Truncate Silence** window is displayed.

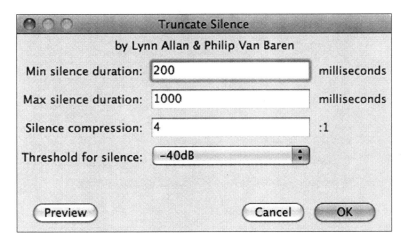

3. Here, you can set the length (minimum and maximum) of the silences you want to shorten or delete.

4. Click on **OK** to see and hear the results!

It is highly recommended that if you have used the **Fade Out** effect in the track already, that you do not also use this effect.

Wahwah

This is a fun effect that mimics the sound of an electric guitar's distortion pedal. When this pedal is connected to a guitar, it alters the tone to create a sound similar to the human voice. It even automatically adjusts the phase of the left and right channels in a stereo recording, so that it sounds as though it travels "across" speakers. Give it a try:

1. Select the audio track you want to edit.

2. From the main menu, select **Effect** and then **Wahwah**. The **Wahwah** window is displayed.

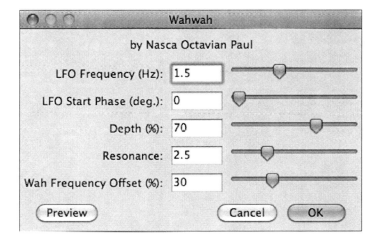

3. Adjust the various settings offered:

   ○ **LFO (Low-Frequency Oscillator) Frequency**—
   The number of times to process the signal in a second

   ○ **LFO Start Phase**—The starting place for the oscillation

   ○ **Depth**—The higher this number the deeper the oscillation sound

   ○ **Resonance**—How "deep" the tones are

   ○ **Wah Frequency Offset**—How much to offset the oscillation sounds

4. Click on **OK** to create the new Wahwah effect in your audio track.

Summary

This chapter was all about audio effects. With over 20 effects in Audacity, we've got a lot to choose from. So we spent the entire chapter reviewing each of the pre-installed effects. We spent a great deal of time discussing how to access and use all of the available effects, and why you might use each of them. This chapter is to be used as a future reference for all of the various effects that Audacity has ready for you, while also getting you ready for the next chapter, in which we will discuss all of the plug-ins, or additions, that you can install with Audacity in order to give you even more effect options.

10
Making Audacity Even Better With Plug-Ins and Libraries

Plug-ins and libraries are extra features that can be added on top of the built-in features of Audacity. Plug-ins can make special sound effects, analyze audio content, or just add to the long list of effects already available in Audacity. Plug-ins are typically used by advanced users of Audacity, or those users who want to add an additional effect to their audio track that can't be found among the pre-installed options.

The most common plug-ins include:

- **Nyquist** plug-ins for audio synthesis and analysis.
- **LADSPA** effect-based plug-ins that can be plugged into a wide range of audio synthesis and recording packages, like Audacity.
- **VST effects,** or Virtual Studio Technology, plug-ins use **Digital Signal Processing (DSP)** to simulate traditional recording studio hardware with software.
- **VAMP** plugins that are for viewing and analyzing the descriptive contents of music audio files. This could be things like histograms or curve data.

Libraries expand the exporting capabilities of Audacity. In Chapter 6, *Saving Projects and Exporting Podcasts*, we discussed and learned how to export an audio track to an MP3 format. There are other libraries as well, and these include:

- LAME
- FFmpeg import/export

Installing plug-ins

Installing plug-ins involves three basic steps: download, extract, and then save the files in the Audacity **Plug-Ins** folder.

1. Go to the Audacity Plug-ins web page. You can find this web site here: `http://audacity.sourceforge.net/download/plugins`.

2. Choose one of the plug-in types, and click on the link appropriate for your operating system, and download the file.

3. Once the file is downloaded, extract it (uncompress) by double-clicking on it.

 For Windows machines, the extracted file will be a `.dll` file.

4. Place the extracted file inside the **Plug-Ins** folder (within the Audacity installation directory).

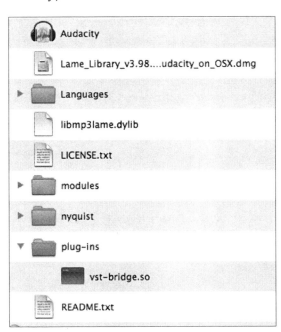

5. Once you save the file, you're all set.

 On Windows computers, the Audacity folder is usually in **Program Files**. On Mac OS X, it is under **Applications**.

6. Restart Audacity. To see all of the new plug-in options, from the main menu, go to the **Effect**, **Generate** or **Analyze** menus. All of the installed plug-ins will be seen below a divider in those menus.

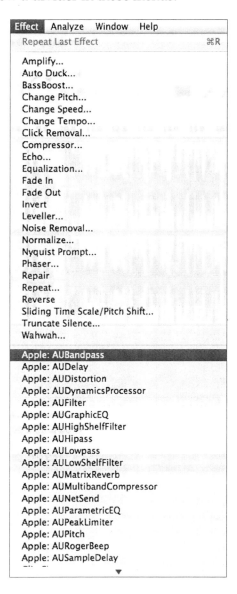

Installing VST Enabler

In order to use any of the VST plug-ins with Audacity, you must first install the VST Enabler.

1. Go to `http://www.audacityteam.org/vst/` and download the install file for your operating system.

2. As with the plug-in installation, after you download and uncompress the file, you need to move it to the **Plug-Ins** folder (within the Audacity installation directory).

3. Restart Audacity, and the VST Enabler will be installed.

Remember, however, that you still need to download and install all VST plug-ins (after downloading and uncompressing them, you need to place them in Audacity's Plug-Ins folder, and then restart Audacity). You will then see these plug-ins in the Effect menu.

Installing libraries

Installing a library is very similar to installing plug-ins. In this example, we'll install LAME, a high-quality MPEG Audio Layer III (MP3) encoder. However the ffmpeg libraries or binaries are also available in the same location. Again, you install in three basic steps: download, extract, and then save the files in the Audacity folder.

1. Open a web browser and go to the LAME download page, here: `http://lame.buanzo.com.ar/`.

2. Find the LAME file appropriate for your computer's operating system and click the link to download the file.

 All of files on this site are accessible, but some browsers, firewall, and proxy combinations cause some downloading issues. Two notes:

1. Use preferred browsers, such as Firefox 3 and above, or Opera.

2. Do not use right-click or control-click to download files, just a standard click will trigger the download.

3. Once downloaded, double-click on the DMG (for Mac computers) or EXE (for windows) file to start the installation.

4. You will be prompted to save the library file, which is called: `libmp3lame.dylib` You can save it anywhere on your computer, but its recommended that you place it in the **Audacity** folder on your computer, so that you remember where to find it when prompted, when you save your first MP3 file.

 For the Windows Operating system, you can usually find the **Audacity** folder in **Program Files**. For Mac OS X, it is in **Applications**.

5. Once you save the **Lame Library** file, you're all set for now. The first time that you try to use this library (or others), you'll be asked to find this `dylib` file.

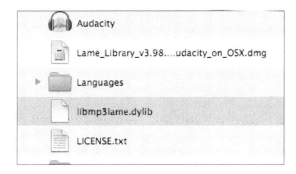

Using a plug-in

You use plug-ins just like the effects that can already be found in the **Effects** menu in Audacity.

When you are ready to use one, you select the area of the audio track on which you want to use this plug in (or select the entire track), and then, from the Audacity main menu, select **Effects**, and then the plug-in of your choice.

Using libraries

In Audacity 1.3.9 there is support for the LAME MP3 encoding (which allows you to export audio tracks in MP3 format) and the FFmpeg import/export library. The latter allows Audacity to import and export additional audio formats, such as AC3, AMR(NB), M4A and WMA. There is also some limited support for importing audio from some video file formats. However, much of this is still in beta form, which means that not all of the features may work fully.

Libraries provide different features than plug-ins—and, for the most part, allow for additional importing and exporting options. Thus, the features are accessed most often through the **File** menu's **Import** or **Export** options.

Summary

Beyond the basics, Audacity allows you to install Plug-ins and Libraries. Both are extra features that can be added into the Audacity software. This chapter explained the basics of plug-ins—how to install them, and where you'll find them once they are installed. The rest is up to you, as you now know all of the basics—and more—for using Audacity to make your own audio tracks.

Toolbar, Menu, and Keyboard Shortcut Reference

After you use Audacity for a while, you might want to start using keyboard shortcuts for your most used features in the software. These are keyboard combinations that are usually easy to remember, and are also faster than using the menus. See the list below to get started!

 If you are using a Mac computer, instead of using the *Ctrl* key, you use the *Command* key in any of the combinations listed next.

Keyboard Shortcut	Feature/Function
Project and Files	
Ctrl + *N*	New project
Ctrl + *O*	Open project
Ctrl + *W*	Close project and Audacity
Ctrl + *S*	Save Project
Ctrl + *P*	Preferences
Tools Toolbar Shortcuts	
F1	Selection Tool
F2	Envelope Tool
F3	Draw Tool
F4	Zoom Tool
F5	Time Shift Tool

Tools Toolbar Shortcuts

F6	Multi-Tool Mode
D	Next Tool
A	Previous Tool

Editing Menu Shortcuts

Ctrl + Z	Undo
Ctrl + Y	Redo (Windows)
Ctrl + Shift + Z	Redo (Mac/Unix)
Ctrl + X	Cut
Ctrl + C	Copy
Ctrl + V	Paste
Ctrl + K or *Delete*	Delete
Ctrl + L	Silence
Ctrl + D	Duplicate
Ctrl + A	Select All
Z	Find Zero Crossings

Navigation, Playback and Recording

Space	Play or Stop
Shift + Space or *L*	Loop
P	Pause
R	Record
1	Preview one second
B	Play from cursor to selection
Ctrl + 1	Zoom In
Ctrl + 2	Zoom Normal
Ctrl + 3	Zoom Out
Ctrl + F	Fit In Window
Ctrl + Shift + F	Fit Vertically
Ctrl + E	Zoom to Selection
Ctrl + I	Import Audio
Ctrl + B	Create Label at current position
Ctrl + R	Repeat Last Effect

B

Glossary of Terms

AIFF, MP3, WAV — these are all common audio file types. You can import or export audio in these formats into and out of Audacity. However, only Audacity will be able to open files of the AUP file type.

Amplify — the process of increasing (or decreasing) volume of an audio track (or a portion of it).

Appending — adding an additional piece of audio at the end of an existing track, or to another project.

Bit or Sample Rates — computers use a unit of measure called bits. Bit or sample rates are the number of computer bits that are processed per unit of time, and are expressed in kilobits per second (kbps), or 1,000 bits per second. The higher bit or sample rate, the better the quality of your recording.

Click — short, disruptive sounds in an audio recording, most commonly heard on vinyl records. These show as spikes in the waveform.

Clip — is a short segment of audio. It can be combined with others to make an audio track.

Control toolbar — contains common icons used for any audio device: Play, Pause, Record, Skip to Start, Skip to End and Stop. These are the basic controls for recording and playing back the sound that you recorded using Audacity.

Decibel (dB) — a measurement of sound. It is a logarithmic unit used to describe the ratio of the signal level. Because it is logarithmic and not linear, its measurement scale doesn't increase by intervals of one. Instead each interval grows by a larger interval than the previous one. For example, a common ratio would be 10, so that the marks on the scale would read: 1, 10, 100, 1000, 10000, and so on.

Effect—artificially created or enhanced sounds, or sound processes used to emphasize certain portions of an audio track. You can *add* or *apply* effects to an audio track.

Editing Toolbar—contains all of the tools available for editing audio tracks in Audacity.

Export—the process of saving audio in another format other than that of the program you created it in. Typically, for audio, you will export in a WAV or MP3 format.

Hertz (Hz)—a unit of measurement used to describe frequency or tone. One single hertz is one audio wave cycle from crest to crest. The human ear can hear frequencies ranging from 20 Hz to 20 kHz.

LAME—an Audacity library plug-in that allows you to encode (or digitize) MP3 files. LAME is a high-quality MPEG Audio Layer III (MP3) encoder.

Library—a collection of audio files or tracks. Can be grouped by content of the audio files (like a music library) or just by the location of where they are stored.

Library Plug-ins—additional software modules that, when installed, expand the exporting capabilities of Audacity. Some libraries let you encode (or digitize) MP3 files, MPEG, and other audio file formats.

Main menu—(in Audacity) provides access to the basic functionality of the Audacity software.

Metadata or Tags—information about the recording, such as the artist or creator name, track title, genre, and album title.

Mixer toolbar—the toolbar in Audacity that is all about volume.

Mixing—the process of combining many tracks of different types of audio into a single recording.

Noise—unwanted sound of any kind, especially unintelligible or dissonant sound that interferes with the main audio in a track.

Normalize—to force all audio tracks to be of the same volume.

Overdubbing—having sound of any kind that plays (or is recorded) over the previously recorded track.

Pitch—sounds or tones are essentially regular, even-spaced waves of air molecules, as we see in the Audacity timeline. Audibly, we notice sounds as being higher or lower than others—this difference in sound is pitch.

Visibly, we see this difference by the spacing of the sound waves; the shorter the wavelength (from top to bottom), the higher the sound or pitch; the longer the waves, the lower the sound. Think of pitches as musical notes (like middle C and F sharp)—each has definite frequencies.

Plug-Ins—are extra features that can be added on top of the features of Audacity. Some plug-ins can make special sound effects or analyze audio content, and others just add to the long list of effects already available with Audacity.

Podcast—a simple audio track that is recorded, exported from a project, and then posted on a blog, or podcast site for downloading by others.

Preferences—are set up when you start a new Audacity project. They define the project's bitrate (quality), how we are going to export it, and what types of devices will be used when we record the project.

Project—when you open Audacity, you will open or create a new project (the AUP file). It includes all of the files, timing, and information on how you combined and edited different pieces of audio in order to make it into your file or project. This term isn't specific to audio editing, but to software that combines pieces of different files into one unit to create a final output.

RSS reader—is an acronym for Really Simple Syndication **(RSS)**. It is type of web format that is used to publish frequently-updated items, such as blog entries, news headlines, audio, and video. If you use an RSS Reader, it checks the RSS feed web addresses regularly for new updates, and then alerts you when new content, such as podcasts, is available.

Sibilant sounds—a sound near or around an "s", "sh", and "ch" that hisses and distracts for the rest of the recording. A sibilant sound can be corrected through the use of proper editing in Audacity.

Silencing—lets you take out noise. Only you aren't actually deleting anything from the timeline, you just silence the noise.

Skype—a software application that lets you make voice and video calls over the Internet. These calls are made to other users of the service for free, or to landlines and mobile phones for a small fee. You can also use Skype for instant messaging, file transfer, and video conferencing.

Tags or Metadata— see *Metadata or Tags*

Tempo—the speed at which the audio track should be played.

Timeline—follows the horizontal of the audio track. Specifically, it shows a measurement of time for the entire length of the track.

Tools toolbar—gives you control options in the recorded audio's timeline. From this toolbar you can select audio, envelope sound, draw, zoom into the timeline, use Time Shift, and use the multi-tool option.

Track—one continuous audio element.

Trim—removes unwanted or "extra" sound from the beginning and end of an audio track.

Transcription toolbar—Contains the tools that let you speed up or slow down audio tracks.

Selection toolbar—this is located at the bottom of the Audacity main window, just below the project window. Its most common use is to set the Project Rate.

Index

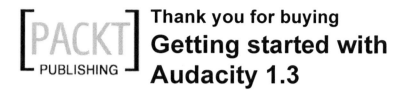
Thank you for buying
Getting started with Audacity 1.3

Packt Open Source Project Royalties

When we sell a book written on an Open Source project, we pay a royalty directly to that project. Therefore by purchasing Getting started with Audacity 1.3, Packt will have given some of the money received to the Audacity project.

In the long term, we see ourselves and you — customers and readers of our books — as part of the Open Source ecosystem, providing sustainable revenue for the projects we publish on. Our aim at Packt is to establish publishing royalties as an essential part of the service and support a business model that sustains Open Source.

If you're working with an Open Source project that you would like us to publish on, and subsequently pay royalties to, please get in touch with us.

Writing for Packt

We welcome all inquiries from people who are interested in authoring. Book proposals should be sent to author@packtpub.com. If your book idea is still at an early stage and you would like to discuss it first before writing a formal book proposal, contact us; one of our commissioning editors will get in touch with you.

We're not just looking for published authors; if you have strong technical skills but no writing experience, our experienced editors can help you develop a writing career, or simply get some additional reward for your expertise.

About Packt Publishing

Packt, pronounced 'packed', published its first book "Mastering phpMyAdmin for Effective MySQL Management" in April 2004 and subsequently continued to specialize in publishing highly focused books on specific technologies and solutions.

Our books and publications share the experiences of your fellow IT professionals in adapting and customizing today's systems, applications, and frameworks. Our solution-based books give you the knowledge and power to customize the software and technologies you're using to get the job done. Packt books are more specific and less general than the IT books you have seen in the past. Our unique business model allows us to bring you more focused information, giving you more of what you need to know, and less of what you don't.

Packt is a modern, yet unique publishing company, which focuses on producing quality, cutting-edge books for communities of developers, administrators, and newbies alike. For more information, please visit our website: www.PacktPub.com.

PUBLISHING

Learning VirtualDub: The complete guide to capturing, processing and encoding digital video

ISBN: 978-1-904811-35-0   Paperback: 212 pages

Get started fast, then master the advanced features of VirtualDub, the leading free Open Source video capture and processing tool

1. This book is available as a free download, scroll down for more information

2. Capture and process broadcast, digital, home, streaming video

3. Cut, paste and edit ads, trailers, clips

4. Demos and walkthroughs of processing sample videos

Drupal Multimedia

ISBN: 978-1-847194-60-2   Paperback: 264 pages

Create media-rich Drupal sites by learning to embed and manipulate images, video, and audio

1. Learn to integrate multimedia in your Drupal websites

2. Find your way round contributed modules for adding media to Drupal sites

3. Tackle media problems from all points of views: content editors, administrators, and developers

Please check **www.PacktPub.com** for information on our titles

Moodle 1.9 Multimedia

ISBN: 978-1-847195-90-6   Paperback: 272 pages

Create and share multimedia learning materials in your Moodle courses.

1. Ideas and best practices for teachers and trainers on using multimedia effectively in Moodle

2. Ample screenshots and clear explanations to facilitate learning

3. Covers working with TeacherTube, embedding interactive Flash games, podcasting, and more

Joomla! 1.5 Multimedia

ISBN: 978-1-847197-70-2   Paperback: 376 pages

Build media-rich Joomla! web sites by learning to embed and display Multimedia content

1. Build a livelier Joomla! site by adding videos, audios, images and more to your web content

2. Install, configure, and use popular Multimedia Extensions

3. Make your web site collaborate with external resources such as Twitter, YouTube, Google, and Flickr with the help of Joomla! extensions

4. Follow a step-by-step tutorial to create a feature-packed media-rich Joomla! site

Please check **www.PacktPub.com** for information on our titles

LaVergne, TN USA
04 February 2011
215301LV00003B/28/P